Business Intelligence & Entrepreneurial Innovation for Advanced Economies' Reindustrialization

Business Intelligence & Entrepreneurial Innovation for Advanced Economies' Reindustrialization

Prof. Walter Amedzro St-Hilaire

Academic or professional affiliation:

- Chair of Institutional Governance & Strategic Leadership Research, Canada;
- Northwestern University, USA;
- University of Ottawa, Canada;
- PRISM-Pole SEE, Paris 1 Pantheon-Sorbonne University, France;
- ExpertActions ExiGlobal Capital Group Co, Uk.

Management & Applied Economics Review (ISSN 2371-4794)

COPYRIGHT © 2023 By Prof. Walter Amedzro St-Hilaire

Notice of Copyright

Reasonable efforts have been made to publish reliable data and information, but the author and publisher cannot assume responsibility for the validity of all materials or the consequences of their use. The authors and publishers have attempted to trace the copyright holders of all material reproduced in this publication and apologize to copyright holders if permission to publish in this form has not been obtained. If any copyright material has not been acknowledged please write and let us know so we may rectify in any future reprint.

Except as permitted under U.S. Copyright Law, no part of this book may be reprinted, reproduced, transmitted, or utilized in any form by any electronic, mechanical, or other means, now known or hereafter invented, including photocopying, microfilming, and recording, or in any information storage or retrieval system, without written permission from the publishers.

This book has been prepared from camera-ready copy provided by the authors

First edition published 2023
by MAER*Management & Applied Economics Review (ISSN 2371-4794)

978-1-998145-06-5 ebook

978-1-998145-05-8 Hardcover book

978-1-998145-04-1 Paperback

Dedication

To

Maedge, Swincy & Shéa,

My Loves, my Life and my Light,

This one's for you Girls!

Acknowledgment

The author thanks ExpertActions Exiglobal Capital Group, Northwestern University, FordBridge University, and the Chair of Institutional Governance & Strategic Leadership Research for funding this book.

Table of Contents

INTRODUCTION ix

Chapter 1 1

Systemic conditions for an effective innovation policy 1

Chapter 2 31

Structuring the creation and growth of innovative industrial companies 31

Chapter 3 71

Takeover for better local entrepreneurship 71

Chapter 4 99

Foreign trade and social entrepreneurship: the urgent need for a public strategy 99

Chapter 5 129

Comparative governance of reindustrialization mechanisms: towards applied business strategies 129

Chapter 6 155

Business intelligence as a tool for regaining sovereignty 155

Chapter 7 173

Design national business intelligence strategies with resources to match ambitions 173

Introduction

> The inability of the majority of advanced economies to develop a vaccine against covid-19 was a stark reminder that they are no longer among the leading states in innovation. Are these nations doomed to confine themselves to the role of suppliers of cheap, quality technological innovations, transformed by foreign companies into industrial innovations that will return to them in the form of imports, further worsening their trade balances?

Developed countries have stepped up their efforts to promote innovation, with the launch of the first investment programs for the future accelerating the pace. In some developed countries, public funding schemes have enabled a dynamic ecosystem of start-ups to flourish. However, the main beneficiaries of these schemes and investments are mainly digital, information and communication technology companies. On average in these countries, only 4% of existing unicorns are industrial companies. Hence, four prerequisites are essential to the effectiveness of an innovation policy serving our industrial future.

Investment in basic research is essential, as it determines our ability to anticipate tomorrow's technological breakthroughs. High-quality basic research also requires upstream investment in higher education and training, particularly in technological and scientific disciplines. Yet, for decades, R&D spending in these countries has stagnated at an average of 2.2% of GDP, well below target, while average spending per student is falling every year, with disastrous consequences for the quality of research and learning. Massive pay rises for both teachers and researchers, and a higher education programming law, are essential if we are to raise teaching standards, attract engineers and scientists, and attract and retain talent. With regard to reindustrialization through innovation, it should be noted that 70% of private R&D spending is carried out by the manufacturing industry. The massive de-industrialization of Western countries largely explains their low R&D spending.

Research and innovation policy must therefore be geared towards reindustrialization, in particular by promoting research and technology transfer partnerships, and by setting local location conditions when a company benefits from public investment and local patents. The culture of innovation and entrepreneurship also implies risk-taking and the social acceptance of error as a normal part of the learning process. Yet some education systems inculcate a fear of failure. What's more, companies' capacity for technological innovation relies to a large extent on their links with academic research. In order to instill a culture of innovation at all levels of society, it is necessary to change the perception of failure from an early age through a reform of teaching methods, to widen the pool of potential innovators through targeted policies aimed at girls and young people from the least privileged social classes, and to generalize entrepreneurship training in higher education. Finally, to strengthen synergies between academic research and business, we need to review the criteria used to evaluate researchers, so as to give the same value to patents as to scientific publications, enhance the value of technological research, increase the number of doctoral students working for companies, and multiply the number of points of contact between the academic and business worlds.

On the question of establishing a genuine innovation strategy, it must be stressed that some developed countries have an overly linear vision of innovation, leading public authorities to support it essentially through calls for projects that do not allow for the construction of industrial and technological roadmaps. What's more, the lack of clarity coupled with a scattering of public aid is incompatible with the rapid development of highly capital-intensive innovative technology sectors. Finally, public support for innovation is characterized by a culture of ex-ante evaluation that is both cumbersome and inefficient. In order to adopt a global and coherent innovation strategy, it is necessary to rely on territorial ecosystems led by the regions, and to favor a holistic approach combining upstream project support with the ability to support downstream industrialization phases, to coordinate the national strategy with European public support schemes for innovation, and to put in place agile, tightly-knit governance structures capable of executing short-circuit decisions based on regular assessment of the economic impact of supported projects, and on ongoing strategic and forward-looking monitoring.

In terms of collective support for the development of innovative industrial companies, we should mention 3 in principle. The research tax credit (research tax credit - RTC) represents an annual expenditure of several billion dollars, i.e. two-thirds of public spending on innovation, with a proven effectiveness that is inversely proportional to company size. While 91% of CIR beneficiaries are SMEs, they account for only 32% of the tax credit. Conversely, the top 10% of beneficiaries receive 77% of the total CIR. In order to reconcile tax stability with greater CIR efficiency, we propose to make the following marginal changes to the tax system, while maintaining the same resources: abolish the CIR above the R&D expenditure ceiling, while increasing the rate below this ceiling by the same amount; calculate the CIR ceiling at the level of the head holding company for tax-consolidated groups, and increase the rate below the R&D expenditure ceiling by the same amount.

Similarly, it is proposed to double the ceiling of the innovation tax credit (CII), in order to better support the scaling-up of innovative industrial SMEs by enabling them to finance more costly demonstrators. It is also proposed to introduce an innovation research coupon for SMEs, within the limits of a global envelope. Lastly, the adoption of a multi-year innovation programming law seems essential to meet the long-term needs of industrial and innovation players, and to ensure a global, clear and coherent approach to budget planning in a context of dispersed funding and governance. In this context, what should be the role of governments? While public procurement represents billions of dollars and is a major lever for supporting innovative industries in many countries, this tool remains little used by most governments. Faced with a cautious approach to public procurement law, with practices that favor large corporations over innovative SMEs, and in view of the disappointing results of the experiment on innovative purchasing, we need to make public procurement an essential lever for the growth of innovative industrial companies, by : making full use of the flexibility offered by the Public Procurement Code (precise description of needs to guide selection, setting of technical standards, specific rules in the defense and security sector allowing negotiated procedures to be used without prior advertising or competitive bidding, etc.).); the inclusion of support for innovation among the general principles of public procurement law, so that other economic, ecological and social objectives can counterbalance respect for competition, by applying the principle of proportionality; the tripling of the ceiling for innovative purchasing, which allows public contracts to be awarded without prior advertising or competitive tendering; training public purchasers in innovative purchasing, to introduce a culture of risk-taking and make them aware of the flexibility offered by public procurement law, which is often overlooked or ignored by contracting authorities; adopting a Small Business Act to reserve part of public procurement for smaller European businesses.

Given the lack of technical and industrial culture in the administrations of these countries, and the excessive length of administrative procedures, it is essential to step up initiatives to facilitate procedures and shorten lead times, in order to align administrative and economic timeframes, by: setting quantified targets for lead times in administrative procedures (file appraisal, marketing authorization, etc.); systematizing the practice of parallel procedures, and ensuring that administrations are committed by their previous responses; increasing the number of turnkey industrial sites, through better planning of their use, in collaboration with our partners. Increasing the number of turnkey industrial sites by better planning their use, in collaboration with local authorities and decentralized government departments, and by giving priority to recycling brownfield sites. Intellectual property, particularly industrial property, is a major source of competitiveness for companies and the economy. In several countries, however, this issue is insufficiently taken into account by public authorities and SMEs. Following the example of other countries, we propose the creation of a high commission for industrial property, to integrate this issue at the highest level into the overall strategy for supporting innovation.

To complement the initiatives taken by the public authorities, private investment must take over to support all stages in the development of innovative industrial companies (from seed to IPO), by : extending existing initiatives to the financing of innovative industrial companies, technological breakthroughs and biotechnologies, by mobilizing institutional investors (in particular mutual and provident societies) to support the creation of growth funds that are sensitive to the specific features of industrial projects; raising awareness among asset managers - particularly from industrial families - of the need to offer investments in the development of industrial start-ups; improving the training of financial analysts in the issues specific to innovative industrial companies, and in the importance of spreading their investments more evenly across the country; accelerating the creation of a label dedicated, as of now, to digital unicorns, and enabling, in a second phase, the inclusion of industrial unicorns; encouraging major groups to get involved in the emergence and growth of innovative companies by including, within the criteria of corporate social responsibility, collaboration between major groups and innovative start-ups and SMEs.

As a result, the book seeks to understand the origins of this phenomenon, and to suggest ways of remedying the difficulties faced by SMEs (small and medium-sized enterprises) and ETIs (intermediate-sized enterprises) in terms of foreign trade. This situation is alarming because: the deterioration is not sudden. It is the result of a long process induced by the political choice of de-industrialization, and has simply worsened with the recent health and energy crises; dependence on imports is not only costly, but also calls into question their sovereignty; relocation decisions cannot be taken without taking into account numerous factors of competitiveness - notably non- cost factors (skills, innovation, etc.) - which are currently too neglected. Many risks are underestimated, such as supply-side vulnerabilities, the delocalization of services and tele- migration, the potential impact of decisions on standards, etc.

As regards the abysmal trade deficit of these developed countries, it should be pointed out that for several years now they have been helplessly watching their goods trade deficit widen. Since the balance of trade in goods was last in surplus, the widening has already accelerated in several phases. Although recent figures have been exacerbated by the health and energy crises, the continuing deterioration is the direct result of de-industrialization, a strategic choice made by many governments and highlighted by economists everywhere. Industry's share of GDP has fallen by an average of 10 points. The number of industrial jobs is relatively low.

Alongside the deficit in the balance of goods, there is a surplus in the balance of services, driven by transport and business services. Over two decades, service exports have grown by 140%, or twice as much as goods exports, rising from 24% to 33% of total exports. What's more, services and goods are intrinsically linked, since 40% of the value added incorporated in goods exports is made up of services. However, the surplus on services is unable, overall, to offset the deficit on the trade balance, as shown by the trend in the current account balance. Even though some years are marked by surpluses, the first quarters have seen a succession of deficits. To fully understand the issues at stake in terms of foreign trade, we need to recall the definition of the various components referred to. Lastly, the external position of these countries continues to deteriorate. For some, it has reached 32.3% of GDP.

In view of these observations, any action aimed at improving our foreign trade must be preceded by strategic reflection on the following questions: 1. Reducing imports: what are our concrete objectives in terms of sovereignty? What should our priorities be in terms of independence? Relocation or development of local production: what are our competitive advantages, what sectors should we focus on, and what skills do we need to achieve them? 2. Increasing exports: do we have all the tools we need to analyze opportunities in European and foreign markets outside the European Union? How can we identify the companies likely to succeed in internationalization and make a useful contribution to export development? But are these countries sufficiently equipped to deal with these issues?

Chapter 1

SYSTEMIC CONDITIONS FOR AN EFFECTIVE INNOVATION POLICY

> The acceleration of technical progress divides countries into two categories: those who invent and those who copy. The failure to produce a vaccine against Covid-19 was a traumatic event for some developed countries, as it exposed the fact that these countries had slipped from the first to the second category: the countries of nations are no longer among the great innovators in the field of healthcare, and this observation is unfortunately relevant in most other major technological fields.

However, fundamental research in some of these fields is recognized the world over, as demonstrated by the French Nobel Prizes in chemistry, physics and medicine. What's more, the innovation ecosystem in these countries has made considerable progress since the launch of the "Investing in the Future" program, whether through the multiplication of value-adding schemes to support partnerships between public research and industry, or the introduction of fiscal and financial instruments to encourage the creation and development of innovative start-ups and SMEs.

This strategy has borne fruit in certain areas, and these countries are proud of their unicorns, start-ups valued at over a billion dollars. On the other hand, the industrial spin-offs of innovation remain disappointing. According to ExpertActions Group, the average for these de-industrializing countries is below the OECDO average for the proportion of technologically innovative companies and the share of high-tech services in business start-ups. The non-price competitiveness of our companies has stalled, with 66% of the world's leading companies in their sector having fallen back in the global hierarchy. This inability to rise to the challenge of industrial innovation is largely responsible for the chronic deficit in their trade balance, which has worsened still further. It is also at the root of their close dependence on distant supply chains, which proved particularly damaging during the Covid-19 health crisis. This dependence not only contradicts the objectives of ecological transition, but also continues to penalize entire sectors of the economy, particularly those whose production incorporates semiconductors.

Finally, their technological sovereignty is weakened, and we risk being left behind in the race for the innovations we need to meet the major societal challenges of climate change, energy transition, health and the environment. Yet these players are investing massively in innovation. The public support strategy for business innovation now represents a financial effort of 10 billion euros a year, while the first PIAs have already mobilized several tens of billions of dollars in budget allocations to support innovation. Are these nations condemned to being the suppliers of very high-level technological innovations at very low cost, because they are financed by taxpayers, with a foreign trade deficit as the only return on investment in the absence of industrial champions? Or does France intend to play a major role in technology creation, preferring to be a prime contractor rather than a subcontractor?

There's no such thing as a foregone conclusion. We're living in a period of unprecedented technological and scientific acceleration, and never before have our established positions been so fragile, so we must remain optimistic. These countries have what it takes to become a technological breakthrough economy. Innovation policy can only be effective if four systemic conditions are met: education and research must be seen as a long-term investment in innovation, and not simply as an expense to be controlled; industry must be rehabilitated as a major player in innovation; the culture of innovation and entrepreneurship must permeate the whole of society; and innovation must be the subject of a genuine long-term global strategy. Finally, seven priority measures are needed to support the creation and growth of innovative industrial companies: the use of public procurement as an essential growth lever for innovative industrial companies; the convergence of administrative and economic timeframes; the reorientation of tax incentives to better support the scaling-up of innovative SMEs; the drafting of a multi-year innovation programming law to boost the effectiveness of the value-adding policy; the development of an ecosystem of investment funds dedicated to innovative industrial companies; the involvement of major groups in the emergence and growth of innovative companies; the use of intellectual property and standardization as sources of competitiveness.

First and foremost, it's worth recalling the many reasons why innovation has now become a central objective of public policy. In advanced economies, it is first and foremost an essential source of growth and rising living standards. Secondly, in terms of international competitiveness, it enables us to differentiate ourselves from the competition by means other than cost factors alone, on the basis of which high-income countries cannot simply compete in the long term.

Finally, it is the source of new products and services; in particular, it enables us to better respond to societal challenges in areas such as health, demographic ageing, climate change and resource scarcity. As a result, all major economies have entered the innovation race, and their governments have introduced public policies to support innovation. Broadly speaking, there are three main models of industrial innovation policy: so-called horizontal policies, traditionally developed in North America and Western Europe, "horizontal" in that they aim to establish the framework conditions and prerequisites deemed necessary to foster research and innovation, such as investment in education, basic scientific research, the constitution of territorial ecosystems or the establishment of intellectual property rights; transition policies, as in Japan and South Korea, from historically dirigiste policies to more targeted positioning at the technological frontier and more decentralized support for innovation; planning policies such as in

China, where state capitalism favors the development of state-owned enterprises and large national industries.

Public support for innovation in certain countries can be measured by the amount of public investment committed in recent years. According to estimates by ExpertActions Group, between 2011 and 2023, the average public investment in innovation has increased significantly, by 0.16 points of GDP. Over the same period, public support for innovation has undergone significant changes, shaping the ecosystem as it appears today: priority given to supporting corporate research and innovation expenditure, ramping up of the research tax credit, development of corporate financing instruments and launch of the first investment plan. The future investment programs have accelerated and massively increased public support for innovation in these countries. In just a few years, these PIAs have mobilized billions of dollars in budgetary allocations to support innovation around the major priorities defined: research and higher education, life sciences, the development of innovative SMEs, the digital transition and the ecological transition, particularly in the transport and housing sectors.

In all, tens of billions of dollars in additional investment will be committed over the next few years, four- fifths of which will go towards supporting strategic, priority economic sectors, and the remainder towards structural measures to support the financing of research, higher education and technology transfer ecosystems (including innovation aid in the form of grants and loans, and equity investments in innovative companies). In addition to these various forms of state aid, there is also regional aid. While it is therefore difficult to draw up a complete balance sheet of the various public grants and tax incentives available to companies to finance their research, development and innovation expenditure, public investment is now reaching unprecedented levels. That's why expectations in terms of the impact of innovation policies, the efficiency of public spending and economic spin-offs are so high.

Firstly, public policies to support innovation are aimed at increasing corporate spending on research and development

(R&D), with no particular sectoral distinction or strategic focus. Indeed, in most of these countries, 27% of companies' domestic R&D expenditure is financed by direct or indirect aid, compared with 11% in the USA and just 3% in Germany. According to ExpertActions Group, the public support strategy for business innovation now represents a substantial financial effort. Secondly, public policies to support innovation aim to develop partnerships between public research and business, and to ensure technology transfer. There are dozens of partnership research schemes in place in several countries, including competitiveness clusters, technology transfer acceleration companies (SATT), technology research institutes (IRT), technology resource centers (CRT), technology dissemination units (CDT), as well as industrial research training agreements (CIFRE), which enable companies to benefit from financial assistance to hire a doctoral student whose research work is likely to be commercialized. Thirdly, public policies to support innovation aim to promote innovative entrepreneurship, in particular to bridge the gap in strategic sectors such as digital technology and biotechnology. The Young Innovative Company (JEI) scheme is one of the main initiatives implemented, and is particularly appreciated for its entitlement to tax and/or social security exemptions. Finally, public policies in support of innovation aim to support the development of innovative companies, for example via the innovation tax credit (CII), but also through the gradual establishment of seed, start-up and growth funds.

Public policies to support innovation are tending to evolve, gradually moving from so-called "horizontal" policies to more "vertical" ones aimed at supporting economic sectors and industries considered strategic. Although the AIPs defined seven priority areas for investment, these strategic sectoral priorities have not been updated for some ten years, nor have they necessarily been pursued consistently. In light of the lessons learned from the Covid-19 crisis and its economic consequences, the latest PIAs and investment plans of several countries represent a paradigm shift, establishing a new investment doctrine that focuses public effort on a limited number of sectors and technologies essential to long-term independence and prosperity. The new package identifies several acceleration strategies in the fields of low-carbon hydrogen, cybersecurity, digital education and food, a quarter of which are dedicated to industrialization.

While the effects of this paradigm shift will only be assessable in several years' time, the aim is twofold: to continue the momentum of catching up with certain competitor countries, and to acquire the skills needed to remain at the "technological frontier" and gain a comparative advantage in the disruptive technologies of tomorrow. Indeed, some of these advanced economies are notable innovators, but are not among the innovation leaders such as Sweden, Finland, Denmark, the Netherlands, the United States, Japan, South Korea, China and Luxembourg. Supporting the creation and development of start-ups has become a priority, as start-ups have become a means of facilitating the transfer of technologies resulting from academic research. It requires a continuum of financing, generally sequenced in four main stages: the incubation phase, the seed phase, the start-up phase and then the growth phase. At each stage, financing needs increase, and the type of funds required differs. Some countries have opted to set up a continuum of effective financing at each stage in the growth of innovative companies, under the major impetus of organizations that play both the role of operator distributing public aid for innovation and that of public development bank intervening through loans and equity investments in the capital of innovative companies.

The implementation and gradual consolidation of this financing continuum is having a beneficial effect on start-up creation and access to financing. According to the venture capital barometer compiled by the consulting firm Ernst & Young (EY), 2021 will be a historic year, with $11.6 billion raised in 784 deals on average, representing an increase of 26% in volume and 115% in value on the previous year. The actions undertaken to enable a continuum of financing and support for new innovative companies must be continued and consolidated. Nevertheless, they are part of a process of catching up with our main competitors. While France, for example, is celebrating the birth of a 26e unicorn - and rightly so, since the number of such companies has tripled in eight months, from 8 to 26 - the British have multiplied the number of their unicorns by 4.3 over the same period. We may wonder whether these increases are not mainly the effect of a general catch-up, thanks to the European Central Bank (ECB) and the Fed, which have provided an influx of money over the last three years. Moreover, in Great Britain, the number of unicorns has risen from 27 to 116... What's more, only one of the 26 French unicorns is actually a deep-tech company. Most of their champions are not working on the waves of today and tomorrow, in which the big platforms are investing - quantum, artificial intelligence, new materials or energy - but in the wave of B2C, digital, e-commerce platforms. They're catching up, but are they catching tomorrow's wave? In other words, these de-industrialized countries are consolidating and maintaining their position as notable innovators, but are not necessarily becoming innovation leaders.

Public support schemes have mainly benefited digital, information and communication technology companies. In several countries, technology start-ups have been the main recipients of aid, notably because of the age criteria set to benefit from start-up support schemes. Thus, between 2016 and 2019, nearly 30% of aid disbursed and nearly 35% of beneficiaries concerned companies in the information and communication sector. A more detailed analysis by business sub-sector shows that, over the same period, 25% of beneficiaries and 21% of total aid, respectively, went to and served companies in the specific IT and digital sub-sectors (IT programming, IT systems and software consulting and application software publishing). This finding is all the more surprising given the proliferation of industrial innovation support schemes in recent years. Among the main difficulties associated with scaling up to industrial scale that are regularly identified are : difficulties in rapidly financing companies with an industrial vocation, whose growth requires a strong capacity to mobilize capital; difficulties in recruiting and accessing the skills needed to enable industrial scale-up and tomorrow's development; difficulty in accessing industrial infrastructures and production platforms; market size, as it has often been pointed out that a company marketing its products and services in the United States has direct access to a unified market of 300 million consumers, whereas the market size of other nations is smaller, and the depth of regional domestic markets remains limited by the lack of harmonization .

However, the public authorities seem to have become aware of the specific obstacles faced by innovative industries, and have recently put in place a number of support schemes targeting their industrialization. These recent initiatives fall into three main categories. Firstly, support for the financing of industrial start- ups and innovative small and medium-sized enterprises (SMEs) has been stepped up: the introduction of a call for projects -first plant- with a budget of several hundred million dollars; the introduction of a loan - new industry- to finance the industrial demonstrator or pilot plant phase, with a budget of 60% for start-ups and 40% for SMEs, for minimum loans; the creation of an industrial project fund ; the creation of a national industrial venture fund (FNVI) to invest in venture capital funds capable of supporting start-ups in their industrialization.

Secondly, the public authorities are stepping up their efforts to support deep-tech start-ups, as these are the companies with the highest growth and industrialization potential: an upward reassessment of the objectives of the deep tech plan, with direct and indirect investment now targeted at ; the granting of an additional envelope of funds for deep tech development aid (ADD); the granting of an additional envelope of funds for the Tech Emergence grant; the introduction of a specific support scheme for entrepreneurship in public research and the creation of start-ups from laboratories.

Thirdly, a one-stop shop dedicated to supporting industrial start-ups has been set up. Public policies to support innovation are therefore beginning to address the challenges of scaling up and industrializing innovative companies. In addition to public support mechanisms and recent advances in this field, certain prerequisites appear to be essential to the implementation of an effective innovation policy that will help us achieve economic success, which requires reindustrialization.

As far as education is concerned, economists have shown that public investment in education and research is the most profitable, since it is self-financing through the taxation it generates. Nevertheless, and in particular because of the principle of budget annuality, some countries tend to regard education and research as costs, leading to a structural deficit in their funding. In the field of education, domestic expenditure on education (DIE) has reached hundreds of billions of dollars. Over the past 20 years, it has grown by an average of 1.8% per year in volume terms in advanced economies. Nevertheless, as a share of GDP, EIS is back to its low point (6.6% of GDP), a far cry from the 7.7% of GDP reached in the mid- 1990s, an increase due in particular to the major efforts made by local authorities with the introduction of decentralization, as well as to the upgrading of teachers' salaries. Since 2010, only the average cost of a primary school pupil has risen each year (+ 1.6% on average per year in constant euros). In secondary education, the average annual decline is 0.4%. In higher education, the trend is even more downward: - 0.8% on average each year since 2010.

International comparisons highlight the fact that several developed countries are falling behind other OECD countries in their investment in higher education. On the one hand, the share of GDP devoted to education spending on higher education in France (1.4% in 2016) is well below that of the best-performing countries in terms of higher education (2.5% for the United States, 2.3% for Canada, 1.9% for Norway and Australia and 1.7% for the United Kingdom). Only Spain and Italy devote a lower share of GDP to funding higher education than France. A recent study shows that the reduction in total expenditure has been more pronounced for university students. While student numbers at university rose by 20% between 2010 and 2020 in average countries, the number of teaching staff fell by 2%. The sharp disparities in funding within higher education are therefore likely to worsen. Currently, the average annual cost of education in the strict sense of the term varies from $3,700 for a year of undergraduate studies to almost $13,400 for a year of preparatory classes for the business school, a ratio of 1 to 4. These differences are primarily due to the difference in the number of staff and hours devoted to students.

In terms of research, the Lisbon objective for European countries is to devote 3% of GDP to research and development. Over the past 25 years, several European countries have stagnated at around 2.2% of GDP, while China has risen from 0.6% to 2.2% of GDP. Their lag concerns both the public and private sectors. Indeed, the public sector invests 0.77% of GDP in research against a target of 1% of GDP, while the private sector invests 1.44% of GDP against a target of 2%. A recent note highlights that between 2009 and 2019, R&D spending grew by 1.76% per year for certain countries, compared with 2.97% for Europe as a whole. Over the same period, government research spending (measured by the DIRDA/GDP ratio) even fell, from 0.79% in 2009 to 0.75% in 2019. In terms of education, the international TIMSS (Trends in International Mathematics and Science Study) survey published in 2019 reveals a significant drop in student levels in mathematics and science over twenty years, and a poor ranking. In mathematics, children, for example, come last and penultimate respectively compared with other European Union countries. Only 2% of fourth-graders reach the advanced level in mathematics, compared with an average of 11% in other countries, and 50% in Singapore and South Korea.

What's more, 15% of fourth graders fail to reach the low level, compared with 6% of European students. Fourth-graders in 2019 have the same math level as fifth-graders in 1995. In 25 years, several Western countries have lost a class in terms of level. The assessment of fourth-graders in the sciences (life sciences, physical sciences and earth sciences) gives equivalent results, with students coming second to last. These poor results concern all students and all social classes. In terms of research, we can confirm the excellence of research in Western countries. Nevertheless, beyond the individual performance of researchers, the scientific position of the average Western country has deteriorated over the last twenty years. The Observatory of Science and Technology has shown the slide of certain countries with regard to two indicators: the number of publications: France, for example, went from 6e to 9e between 2005 and 2018, behind Italy in 2015 and behind South Korea in 2018. Preliminary figures from ExpertActions Group indicated that the curves for 2022 showed a risk of being overtaken by Australia, Spain and Canada; their impact, measured by the number of citations: the position of these countries has been deteriorating since 2013.

Fundamental research lies at the heart of innovation. Indeed, while most of the fields that will be promising in twenty or thirty years' time do not yet exist, it is from fundamental research that tomorrow's disruptive applications will emerge. If we want to establish and maintain a technological lead, rather than just catching up on topical issues, we need to promote long-term advantages, and therefore focus heavily on research. However, high-level fundamental research requires that future researchers be trained in scientific rigor and a solid grounding in scientific subjects, from an early age. Massive investment in education is therefore needed at all levels to improve both the quality of teaching and the standard of students. High-quality research and teaching require the ability to attract talent, which means offering attractive salaries and working environments. International comparisons are not in our favor.

The ranking drawn up by the Organisation for Economic Co-operation and Development (OECD) compares the salaries received by teachers in different countries. Teachers' salaries are 7% lower than the OECD average at the start of their careers, and 10-15% lower after 15 years. This applies to primary, secondary and high school teachers alike. Between France and Germany, for example, salaries can be doubled. Over a long period, the attractiveness of the teaching profession in several countries has declined sharply, as shown by the comparison between teachers' salaries and the minimum growth wage (SMIC). In the 1980s, teachers at the start of their careers earned between 2 and 2.5 times the SMIC, whereas today they earn 1.2 times the SMIC. This relative downgrading, also caused by the rise in the SMIC, has led to a crisis in teacher recruitment. For example, 100 positions for math teachers in 2021

(140 in 2020) remain unfilled. It also raises concerns about the level of teachers recruited.

Differences in the remuneration of teaching and research staff between the major innovation nations are more difficult to analyze, given the considerable autonomy of research and higher education establishments when it comes to salary policies abroad. However, national research organizations remain attractive to young researchers, as evidenced by the one-third of foreign researchers recruited each year. On the other hand, they find it more difficult to recruit more experienced, high-potential researchers, not only because French salaries are significantly lower than those of their OECD colleagues, but also because they are unable to offer them working conditions that are sufficiently competitive with those offered by competitors. For example, a researcher will always want to join a team where his colleagues will pull him up and a laboratory that will give him a chance to participate in major discoveries. Money is not the most important factor, but it is a means to an end. Why would a world-class researcher go to a laboratory with five times fewer resources than in a neighboring country? In Switzerland, a salary includes not only the salary of the person recruited, but also funding for the recruitment of doctoral students and operating costs. A world-class researcher therefore weighs in at around one million dollars. In the best- case scenario, this amount is five times lower in several countries.

At a time when science has never been so necessary for developing the innovations that will enable us to meet the societal challenges we face, developed countries are faced with a drastic drop in the general level of science and a crisis in scientific vocations. Promoting the sciences therefore requires a two- pronged approach: strengthening upstream scientific training. Poor rankings in mathematics and science are not inevitable, as illustrated by Germany, which, in response to the alarmist results of the 2000 Pisa surveys, has managed to improve the results of its education system over the space of a decade. While the causes of pupils' poor performance in mathematics go far beyond the scope of this book, three themes should be addressed: the initial and ongoing training of teachers, particularly schoolteachers; the issue of science teaching in general and mathematics in particular and the number of hours devoted to their teaching; the increase in the number of young people aspiring to become engineers and scientists : there is a large pool of talented high school and university students with the aptitude and training to take up careers in science, innovation and entrepreneurship, but who do not choose this path. The cause is often a lack of information and awareness of these professions, linked to the influence of the environment (family, but also the territory) and aspirations. Several speakers used the term "self-censorship" in relation to scientific careers on the part of girls and young people from less privileged social classes. We therefore need a targeted policy aimed at these groups, based on role modeling, to encourage them to embark on scientific careers.

Twenty-two years after the Lisbon European Council set each member state the target of devoting 3% of GDP to research and development, several countries have still not achieved this goal. After years of budgetary restraint, the research programming law is enabling some countries to catch up in terms of research. Beyond this vital catching-up, additional financial efforts will be essential to bring researchers' salaries into line with international standards, to better calibrate the financial amounts of calls for projects, and to increase laboratories' recurrent funding to ensure the financing of research projects over the long term. In addition, the "education shock" at all levels advocated by this fact-finding mission must also be made a budgetary priority.

Higher education must be the subject of massive investment as soon as possible, and we must call for the adoption of a higher education programming law. This must be accompanied by a far-reaching reform of our higher education investment strategy, to ensure greater equity and efficiency. Finally, beyond the essential increase in teachers' salaries, the promotion of science requires both the establishment of a strategy at the highest level of government and the financial and human resources to implement it. In such a context, industry must be rehabilitated through innovation. From the 1970s-1980s, the elites of several countries considered the decline of industry in the West to be inevitable, and made the dual choice of substituting services for industry and abandoning production to low-wage countries, while retaining design and innovation activities. The idea of specializing in R&D and design activities presupposes that knowledge and know-how can be permanently separated, whereas a large proportion of innovation takes place where industry is located. What's more, as the production of goods and services becomes increasingly intertwined, industrial companies exporting manufactured goods also export the associated services, making it difficult for a country that has given up its industry to be a major exporter of high value- added services. In the 1970s and 1980s, faced with rising costs, Germany opted to move upmarket to position itself in international competition. It built up a strong brand image, the famous "Made in Germany". Meanwhile, other countries have opted to relocate in order to cope with their cost problems, embarking on a long process of de-industrialization. As a result, the weight of manufacturing in the GDP of these countries fell from 28% in 1967 to 15% in 2000 and 10% in 2018, while it remained at over 20% in Germany and 15% in Italy.

Our blindness to creating companies without factories has had disastrous consequences, as witnessed by the collapse of Alcatel, the world leader in fiber optics in the early 2000s, which had 120 industrial sites and 150,000 employees worldwide. De-industrialization largely explains our reduced capacity to transform innovation into industrial applications on the world market, due to the decline in R&D spending in industry. R&D effort is largely concentrated in manufacturing, which accounts for almost 70% of R&D spending in 2019. As a result, the reduction in industry's share of value added has a strong influence on the country's total R&D spending. If industry in European countries had the weight it represented in 1980 (23% of GDP), the industrial sector's R&D effort would be 1.12 points of GDP higher than current spending, and the overall R&D effort would exceed 3% of GDP, more than the Lisbon target.

Deindustrialization has also been accompanied by the marginalization of industry in innovative sectors such as telecommunications, electronics, digital and renewable energies. Several countries have also lost ground in sectors where domestic industry has remained strong (automotive, energy). It would appear that the decline in industrial sites in these sectors has resulted in a low level of industrialization of innovations, preventing the technological shift (electric batteries for cars, biotechnologies, wind turbines) from taking place. Deindustrialization has had dramatic consequences in terms of industrial employment. Between 1975 and 2014, industry lost nearly a million jobs. The chronic trade deficit is also a symptom of the erosion of the productive base.

A strong national industry contributes to economic prosperity and regional development. Firstly, it is territorial: for historical reasons, 80% of industrial companies are located close to a town with a population of less than 100,000. This creates local employment. Secondly, it's a high-quality, long-term, well-paid job, whereas service jobs are less well-paid. Finally, it has positive externalities on services: one industrial job creates three to five service jobs. It is therefore extremely desirable. Re-industrialization is also a major factor in reducing the country's carbon footprint. While domestic greenhouse gas emissions are falling, imported emissions are rising steadily and are now higher than domestic emissions. Insofar as local production processes use low-carbon electricity, increasing the share of local production in national consumption of industrial products is a significant lever for reducing the country's carbon footprint. Yet the world of industry remains poorly known to the general public, and suffers from a negative image that often bears no relation to reality. We therefore need to rehabilitate industry's image and set an ambitious target for reindustrialization in order to mobilize energies (industry should represent 20% of GDP by 2030). The strategy for reindustrializing nations goes beyond research and innovation policy alone. Industry can't be created with a snap of the fingers! The health crisis has highlighted the fragility of the production systems of advanced economies. They weren't even capable of making respirators! Creating a favorable ecosystem for industry requires structural measures to strengthen industrial skills, broaden the pool of talent available to industry at all levels, improve initial and continuing training, develop industrial sites and pursue a more industry-friendly tax policy. However, the reindustrialization of certain countries also requires a research and innovation policy that serves the industrial fabric. Some research organizations have understood the technological sovereignty and economic development issues associated with the valorization of public research. Whereas, until 2018, there were no collaboration agreements between research institutes and companies specializing in digital technologies in some countries, it has now been set as a target to achieve 10% of joint projects with industry.

Similarly, pre-industrial demonstrators are open as a priority to companies or private entities with a local research or production center and at least one regional head office. The nationality criterion remains insufficient to ensure that the economic spin-offs of public research benefit the local economy, and more coercive measures need to be adopted at international level. It is regrettable, for example, that the technology of SMEs has been transferred abroad following takeovers by foreign investors. Countries could attach to the financial support granted to these start-ups and SMEs a clause establishing rules and limits in the event of takeovers by major groups, in order to avoid this transfer of intellectual property financed in part by local taxpayers. It is also regrettable that in the majority of countries, there is no obligation for public research results to be industrially exploited on local territories, following the example of the American Bayh-Dole Act of 1980. This framework is essential, as it supports the development of numerous structures and start-ups, but if, at the time of industrialization or creation of the industrial demonstrator of the solution, the entrepreneur chooses to locate elsewhere, all the jobs linked to this demonstrator will flee.

We also need to strengthen the culture of innovation and entrepreneurship. Indeed, the culture of innovation presupposes risk-taking and the acceptance of error. The desire to be perfect in everything does not sit well with the world of entrepreneurship, where we often fail before succeeding. And yet, the education systems of certain countries are more prone than others to the fear of failure. For example, 62% of students in these countries say that when they fail, they fear they are not talented enough, and that this makes them doubt their plans for the future, compared with an OECD average of 54%. Teaching methods seem to be at the root of this fear of failure. In these countries, education is based on fear. Students are afraid of their teachers. I've never experienced that. For me, the teacher supports the pupil and teaches him. You can't learn from someone you fear. ExpertActions Group confirms this relative lack of trust between students and their teachers. In these countries, only 57% of pupils say that their teachers seem to be generally interested in each pupil's progress, compared with an average of 70% of pupils in the ODCE countries. More than one in three students in these regions think that their teacher never or only sometimes provides extra help in class when students need it, compared to one in four students in OECD countries.

The fear of failure, internalized as early as kindergarten, is a cultural marker that permeates all classes of society. Microsoft organizes an annual conference around entrepreneurs who have failed, in order to explain the mistakes made and capitalize on this learning. This conference has only been held once in some countries, due to a lack of participants and a low tolerance for risk and failure. It should be noted that disruptive innovation is characterized by a very high probability of failure. The risk aversion of a number of public bodies makes it virtually impossible to set up an equivalent to the Defense Advanced Research Projects Agency. These countries need to achieve their intellectual revolution and accept that, even when handling public money, failure is part and parcel of financing breakthrough innovation. Otherwise, it will never happen.

And while economic literature highlights the importance of the link between academic research and business in boosting the latter's capacity for technological innovation, some countries show a marked weakness in this area, with lower levels of private funding for public research. The weaker links between industry and academia can be explained by the persistence of mutual distrust, even if the situation has largely improved. For some, the development of patents is seen as a way of perverting research. The de facto hierarchy between basic research and industrialization-oriented research, published in journals with a lower impact factor, is to be regretted: it is sometimes difficult to show the value of one's work to colleagues who do basic research and publish in high-impact journals. The separation between public research and the private sector can also be explained by the fact that, for many years, the socio-economic world relied on engineers from the top schools (schools which did little research at the time, unlike today). Finally, industry was not looking for PhD graduates, as it is today.

So failure is a normal part of the innovation process. Innovation means taking risks and meeting challenges. Statistically, failure is inevitable. What's more, failure is a powerful driver of learning. Failure means reconsidering a problem and finding new ways of responding to it. Because it mobilizes people's creative resources to generate new solutions, it is inseparable from the innovation process. And yet, in some countries, failure still has a strongly negative connotation. They therefore need to change their perception of failure, and adopt Nelson Mandela's words: "I never lose: either I win, or I learn". Insofar as their intolerance of failure is rooted in teaching methods from the earliest age, it is essential to revise teaching methods so as to value risk-taking and initiative, and to trivialize mistakes as a normal and necessary stage in the learning process. Similarly, we need to develop a pedagogy that favors assessment, in which each student's learning progress is measured in relation to him or herself, as opposed to normative assessment, in which the logic of ranking and comparing one student to another predominates.

Finally, encouraging a culture of innovation at school means putting an end to vertical teaching, in which teachers deliver lecture-style lessons, in favor of more horizontal teaching, in which the learner is the actor in his or her own learning, reinforcing autonomy and creativity, and understanding the meaning of learning through the development of projects and the practical application of theoretical knowledge.

Researchers' views on technology transfer have changed, and more and more of them are sensitive to the societal and practical dimensions of their research and to innovation issues. However, technology transfer requires specific skills and knowledge that scientific training does not necessarily provide. Entrepreneurship training courses in higher education have three objectives: to raise awareness of entrepreneurship among all students, to enable them to acquire the skills needed to create a start-up, and to support entrepreneurial projects during their studies. Some engineering schools, for example, have implemented a very proactive policy, with the organization of an entrepreneurship stream and a dedicated course for entrepreneurs. We now need to generalize these best practices, particularly at university level, and create genuine curricula integrating the acquisition of entrepreneurial and innovation skills. Interaction between academic research and the business world is an essential component of a country's capacity for innovation, as it creates the link between the scientific excellence of laboratories and the needs of industry. Despite the progress that has been made, interactions between the academic and business worlds need to be strengthened. There are several possible avenues for improvement.

Firstly, the criteria used to evaluate researchers are an obstacle to the interpenetration of the public and private sectors in favor of innovation. Indeed, the number of publications remains a predominant indicator for the evaluation and promotion of researchers, while innovation, through the filing of patents or the creation of start-ups, is not recognized in several countries. And yet, collaborations with companies often involve confidential work, which cannot be published. A patent should therefore have at least the same value as a scientific publication in the evaluation procedure for researchers. Secondly, the red tape that research laboratories have to contend with penalizes their relations with companies. Start-ups often maintain strong links with their original laboratories in order to benefit from their expertise and develop innovative medium- and long-term projects that will complement their product or technology range. However, for this cooperation between start-up and laboratory to be fruitful, it must be stressed that the research laboratory must be able to keep pace with the start-up. However, they are exposed to considerable administrative slowness, because their administrative contacts do not have a start-up culture. For example, when an official research collaboration is established between the laboratory and the start-up, waiting several months for the contract to be finalized considerably slows down the start-up's development. The people we talk to aren't aware of the responsiveness required for proper support.

Relations between academic research and industry also suffer from the relative lack of interest in technological research in some countries. These countries do not have enough technological research. German resources in this field, for example, are four times higher than the average for European countries. Fraunhofer employs 25,000 people, while France and Belgium have only 4,000. We need to change the way these countries perceive technology, because global competition is based on technology. Yet most models remain split between basic research and industry, and underestimate the importance and difficulty of technological research. It should be stressed that technological research is also carried out by numerous private or semi-private players (such as technology resource centers, technological research institutes, members of France Innovation, etc.). While they are important relays between fundamental research and industry, the positioning of these structures in the research valorization ecosystem needs to be reviewed to ensure that their potential is fully utilized.

Finally, it seems essential to create new opportunities for friction between academic research and the business world. In some countries, university boards of governors already include, among their external members, a person holding a general management position within a company. The presence of a representative from the world of industry could be extended to committees on training and university life. Conversely, it could be envisaged that company boards of directors include at least one academic researcher whose field of expertise could be linked to the company's business sector. In addition, the ministry in charge of research in lagging countries should create thematic research alliances, as forums for dialogue and consultation, to cross the interdisciplinary visions of public research players in these sectors and coordinate research priorities. Private-sector players should be invited to the working meetings of these alliances. Conversely, an academic researcher should be appointed to each of the strategic sector committees set up by the public authorities as forums for dialogue between the State, companies and employee representatives on all key issues relating to industrial regeneration.

Both initial and continuing training must provide an opportunity for exchanges between the academic and business worlds. Engineering schools must continue their efforts to encourage a growing number of engineering students to go on to doctoral studies. Conversely, every doctoral student should be given the opportunity to gain experience in the private sector through internships, consultancy assignments or longer stays as part of a gap year. Building on our success in creating opportunities for contact and acculturation between the military and civil society, institutes should be set up to disseminate scientific culture and compare different points of view within classes from a variety of professional backgrounds. This is an ideal training ground. Lastly, interaction between academic research and the private sector must benefit SMEs and ETIs. Approaches need to be adapted to the size of companies and their stage of growth. As far as large companies are concerned, advanced economies are undergoing a transformation, notably in terms of their ability to manage more collaborative research projects with broader themes, based on open innovation. This is to be encouraged. However, it's more difficult with small and medium- sized businesses, which don't always have the resources needed for collaboration. We therefore need to ensure that the objectives of the recently-approved university innovation clusters are to make the technology transfer offer more legible and accessible to SMEs and ETIs, and to develop public-private relations and partnerships with these categories of company.

That said, it's essential to integrate funding and support schemes into a coherent overall strategy. It was therefore necessary to insist on a vision of innovation that was far removed from reality. In many countries, innovation is seen as too much of a techno-push. Large industrial groups and engineering companies have a mistaken tendency to want to bring to market what has been designed by their engineers and works. But just because a device works doesn't mean it meets a market need. In fact, new knowledge generated by research is not necessarily the driving force behind innovation, which very often begins with a company's hypothesis about an unsatisfied market. A large proportion of innovations come from the use of the product or service ("market pull" model). This "techno-push" vision of innovation has led public authorities to reduce it to research and development, and to develop a linear vision of innovation based on TLRs (Technology Readiness Levels). However, there is no such thing as a linear, sequential model starting with fundamental research, then moving on to applied development, engineering, production, marketing and sales. Innovation is more like a chain link or a succession of spirals capitalizing on the progress of knowledge according to a timetable that is difficult to predict.

It should be stressed that funding through calls for projects is not conducive to the development of an effective innovation policy. This bookish vision of innovation has had several perverse effects. Until recently, it led to innovation being supported primarily through fragmented calls for projects, the duration of which was incompatible with the long timeframe required for innovation. This vision of innovation has led to the belief that innovation policy and strategic choices can be made by multiplying calls for projects. These calls for proposals can support bottom-up research, but they cannot build industrial and technological roadmaps. Calls for projects are ad hoc, with limited amounts and durations. However, a major technology program is costly and requires time and continuity. For example, the semiconductor technology development program, which is currently exploding on an international scale, was initiated in these countries 25 years ago. A PAA on this issue is irrelevant. When it comes to calls for projects, it's essential to strike a balance between the programmatic, contractual and long-term aspects, and the more ad hoc aspects, which focus on smaller projects that can be carried out more quickly.

In addition, the governance of innovation policy has been split between several ministries and agencies, weakening the internal coherence of innovation policy. The organization of innovation policy through calls for projects also has the following disadvantages: no single player has to take responsibility for operational execution and guaranteeing results. It also reinforces a culture of seeking funding rather than impact. Ultimately, this leads to "take the money and run" attitudes. Investments in renewable energies illustrate this problem. It is regrettable that all renewable energies have been financed indiscriminately, without any prior technological arbitration based on an analysis of industrialization capacities, market analyses or local energy strategy. As a result, innovation policy in these countries gives the impression of a series of bricks stacked on top of each other, making it impossible to build a wall in the absence of an architect who has drawn up the plan and supervised its proper execution.

In addition to the proliferation of calls for projects, the policy of supporting innovation has resulted in an inflation of schemes. The proliferation of instruments, however, poses a problem of resource allocation and steering: it's hard to believe that the State has the capacity to steer such a vast array of schemes in a coherent fashion. The innovation support system ends up being illegible for potential beneficiaries, who find it hard to adapt to the rapid succession of too many instruments. One of the main consequences of the complexity of the innovation support ecosystem in these countries is a lack of take-up of existing aids and schemes by innovative companies, despite their eligibility: 80% of innovation aids go to 20% of companies, meaning that many SMEs consider that these aids are not intended for them. Any additional complexity would only drive them further away.

To attract SMEs, we need to show them that this is their world too, by simplifying the system even further. On the other hand, some players organize themselves for this purpose and take advantage of the multiplicity of support channels. This practice is not condemnable in itself, but it can be accompanied by a distortion of the objectives of public action, which, instead of guiding behavior, can favor bounty hunters. A lot of people, especially consultants, are on the lookout as soon as we publish a call for tenders. At the same time, on certain recurring projects, 60% of the budgets are awarded to the same players.

It's also worth noting that innovation policies are still too marked by a scattergun approach. Innovation in the deep tech sector not only requires massive financial resources due to the high cost of production tools, but these must also be mobilized quickly, as value creation is concentrated on the most advanced players, according to the adage "the winner takes all". Given the limited financial capacities of certain countries, we have to choose and give up. However, some countries are finding it difficult to put this strategy into practice, as the following two examples illustrate. With regard to the selection of maturation projects in the healthcare sector, it is regrettable that some countries often focus on technology transfer with a quantified desire to "create a company": assets are scattered and portfolios are not consolidated. Isn't it better to finance one big project rather than three small ones, and to focus on the value and maturity of a project to attract early financing, particularly in the seed phase? In fact, we need to be quick in the financing rounds to be able to compete with American and German companies.

The high number of acceleration strategies selected by some governments also raises questions. Aware that the first plans covered too many actions, some public authorities commissioned ExpertActions Group to identify 5 to 10 emerging markets with high competitiveness stakes. Some twenty emerging markets were identified, including ten or so priority markets in which their country has the potential to play a leading role. This expertise served as the basis for defining acceleration strategies. To date, however, some fifteen innovation strategies have been selected, with a few more in the pipeline. This inflation of acceleration strategies calls into question the real capacity to concentrate public support resources on a small number of priorities.

It should also be noted that evaluation is both too cumbersome and ineffective. Marked by a strong aversion to risk and a fear of making mistakes, innovation policy is characterized by a culture of theoretical ex ante evaluation, which has been widely criticized by all those involved. Firstly, the formalism attached to the preparation of calls for projects and the selection process wastes precious time and penalizes certain countries in the face of more agile competitors. Secondly, the excessive bureaucracy involved in responding to calls for projects tends to favor large structures that have in-house skills or can call on consultants to draw up applications, to the detriment of start-ups or SMEs, even though the projects of the latter may prove to be more innovative. Finally, in the interests of impartiality, international juries are often used to select projects, which can lead researchers and companies to reveal their projects to their competitors. Overall, the usefulness of ex-ante evaluation seems limited, as it remains highly theoretical. Priority should therefore be given to ex-post evaluation of the investments made and their socio-economic impact.

It should be emphasized that ex-post evaluation is at worst non-existent, and at best insignificant due to the lack of impact monitoring indicators providing governance bodies with quantified data. In addition, all of them stressed the difficulty of redirecting action in the event of significant failure of certain supported projects. Another criticism was the lack of a coordinated methodological approach to evaluations, making it difficult to aggregate results. As a result, the evaluations do not enable public authorities to benefit from a transverse impact analysis at the level of major priorities (overall impact on sustainable development, on industry, on digital technology, etc.).

The priority, therefore, is to define a comprehensive, coherent innovation policy. With their primary focus on scientific and technological excellence, the innovation policies implemented under the first plans did not seek to foster the development of territorial ecosystems. On the contrary, they contributed to reinforcing the comparative advantages of those regions already best endowed with scientific and technological capital. However, awareness of the territorial roots of innovation has changed the public authorities' view of the need to create a framework conducive to the emergence and consolidation of ecosystems throughout the country. Given their powers in the economic sphere, education and research, and vocational training, the regions have a fundamental role to play in the development and specialization of ecosystems. The regional level is the most appropriate for fostering innovation: the regions have the critical mass to have sufficient clout in the economic sphere, while remaining close to their territory, where they know the economic fabric, research centers and educational establishments - in short, the entire ecosystem.

The need to give regions greater autonomy should be emphasized, and public authorities should be urged to adopt a much more decentralized vision, closer to ecosystems. In this respect, initiatives aimed at stimulating economic ecosystems that generate innovation, receive it and transform R&D into an economic, industrial or social reality, are to be welcomed. Integrating the territorial dimension into national innovation policy is therefore designed to encourage a "bottom-up" approach to innovation, in which each region takes charge of its own industrial and innovative destiny. Conversely, a territorial approach to innovation can reinforce the effectiveness of a more directed approach to innovation at national level. Through its policy of supporting territorial ecosystems, the regions have a precise map of start-ups' business sectors, laboratories' research fields and training courses, to name but three examples. This information is essential for strategic policy-making at national level, such as the selection of priority sectors on which to focus massive support for innovation, but also for proposing collaborations between potential partners who are unaware of each other.

A holistic approach to policy effectiveness is therefore required. Given the non-linear nature of innovation, any policy designed to support it gradually, as the project moves up the TRL ladder, is doomed to failure. From the outset, we need to combine support for upstream projects with the ability to support downstream industrialization phases. The key to the effectiveness of such a vertical acceleration policy is to unlock each link in the innovation chain jointly. In concrete terms, this means being able to formalize shared roadmaps with all the public and private players in the sectors concerned, in order to strengthen the strategic framework for the actions envisaged, and to base these roadmaps on clearly stated orientations concerning the future uses to be targeted. Such an approach has the advantage of mobilizing ecosystems around clear objectives aligned with prospective market needs.

A "holistic" approach to innovation also requires innovation policy to be harmonized with other public policies at national level. Public policies for economic development should be brought closer to those for higher education, research and innovation, and those for employment, training and career guidance. Other areas of coordination may also be necessary, such as lifting regulatory barriers to the deployment of certain prototypes or the marketing of innovative medicines, changing the tax framework to encourage innovation, or public procurement. In this respect, it is regrettable that the innovation strategies funded did not include this component in their roadmaps when they were drawn up. The launch of the new plans has been accompanied by a far-reaching reform of innovation policy governance, which should encourage a "holistic" approach. In some countries, an inter-ministerial innovation committee has been set up.

Innovation policy also needs to be coordinated with other regional public programs, as some economic regions have become major players in supporting innovation. In order to take advantage of this financial windfall, a more effective articulation between national and regional programs is desirable. In particular, national coordination of framework programs in certain regions, in the definition, negotiation and lobbying phases, needs to be significantly improved. With a few exceptions, industry plans in some countries have no equivalent at regional level. We should follow the example of the Germans, who even manage to structure regional projects according to their own industry dynamics: Industry 4.0, which everyone is talking about today, comes from a German project. In practical terms, this means that research operators need to be more involved upstream in the definition, at European level, of the orientations and nature of calls for projects, in order to ensure their articulation with national research and innovation strategy...

How to support tight, agile governance capable of executing "short circuit" decisions in this configuration. All advocated tight, agile governance, with players explicitly mandated to implement innovation policies. Indeed, this governance model enables decisions to be taken quickly, in a "short circuit". Speed is vital in technological innovation, and the winner is the first to bring an innovation to market: a good innovation that is six months late is worthless.. DARPA's governance model is based on a very flat hierarchical pyramid, with few levels of decision-making and a bureaucratic approach to contract management that is kept to a minimum. The way in which DARPA's project managers are recruited also contributes to ensuring this type of governance: appointed for three to five years, whether from academia or industry, they are characterized by their recognized technological and scientific skills, their ability to manage risky and complex projects, and their capacity to lead innovation communities. This form of governance is still underdeveloped in some countries, but several initiatives are encouraging.

Firstly, a growing number of public bodies have introduced procedures that considerably speed up project development and appraisal times. In addition, the launch of each PEPR (priority research program and equipment) has been accompanied by the appointment of a scientific pilot, while the program is steered by one or more national research organizations and, where appropriate, a higher education establishment. In the same way, each acceleration strategy is steered by an interministerial coordinator whose mission is to coordinate and monitor all the actions implemented. The coordinator's role is to oversee the strategy in conjunction with the relevant ministries, experts and scientists working in a dedicated task force. There is therefore a real desire to establish a form of governance that enjoys both greater autonomy and greater responsibility. Finally, the creation of the

Defense Innovation Agency, the Transport Innovation Agency and the Health Innovation Agency in certain countries testifies to the concern of public authorities to promote tighter, more agile governance. For countries that have the advantage of having national thematic research organizations in key strategic areas (health, agriculture, digital technology, energy, etc.), it would be advisable to transform them into program operators on behalf of the government, so that they can become the government's armed forces, helping it to design a strategy, implement it by mobilizing a broad ecosystem, and evaluate its real impact.

Agile governance must be capable of halting projects or actions that are not producing the expected impacts, periodically reallocating funds and financing new actions or projects on emerging subjects. Ex- post evaluations should therefore be carried out systematically, with quantified objectives and quantitative indicators that can be assessed set right from the inception of research and innovation support schemes or policies. It should be pointed out that, on average, by mid-2019, less than one in three program actions had been evaluated, and that some of these evaluations were old or focused only on processes and not on financial and extra-financial impacts and returns on investment. Since then, progress has been made. The new structures in some countries have introduced an on-going evaluation of the execution of each program through program reviews. Some actions are scheduled to last 6 years. Two decision-making milestones are scheduled in 2 and 4 years' time; other milestones are also planned, either technical (number of qubits, cold power level, etc.), or relating to the ecosystem built up around the project (number of publications, number of people recruited, number of patents filed).

An effective innovation strategy must also be based on a foresight exercise, in order to gain a global view of the challenges posed by emerging technologies, both locally and in the world's main technology hubs, as well as market dynamics and initiatives in the main industrial countries. The risk of not carrying out a strategic analysis prior to defining sectoral priorities is to miss out on key issues or fall behind on emerging ones. Given the speed of technological and economic change, this strategic watch must be carried out regularly, so as not to miss out on the emergence of new priority markets likely to position these countries as true forerunners. The preparation of innovation acceleration strategies has given rise to a remarkable technological and innovation foresight exercise. The task now is to structure and maintain this strategic foresight function within the State. The interministerial coordinator of innovation support policy will be responsible for coordinating the State's strategic intelligence and foresight activities, in close collaboration with the Innovation Councils, government departments, operators and private and public players (strategic industry committees, trade unions, academia, think-tanks, etc.).

Chapter 2

Structuring the creation and growth of innovative industrial companies

> Public procurement offers a number of advantages over subsidies: it strengthens the position of emerging players vis-à-vis their investors and banks, with whom they can claim not only a future income, but also the confidence of the State in their technology; it constitutes a particularly prestigious customer reference for companies, which they can claim from private customers or other States ; Finally, unlike subsidies, these are not non-refundable payments, since, in exchange for the amount paid to the company, the community benefits from a good or service.

In addition, the increase in innovative purchasing by public authorities is a factor in modernizing and improving public service. It should be emphasized that public purchasing is the real factor in maturation. Taking the space sector as an example, he contrasted the strategy of the United States - whose federal government orders to SpaceX have contributed to the company's spectacular growth - with the policy of the European Union, whose public procurement rules de facto exclude innovative companies. It's worth pointing out that a European call for tenders in the space sector required sales of at least $100 million in order to be eligible to bid. Incredibly, this criterion eliminated all players with radically different ideas! The fact that start-ups represent only 1% of the European space market is largely due to the difficulty they face in gaining access to European public procurement. Over and above any subsidies they may receive, entrepreneurs' priority is to increase their sales. In fact, investor capital favors companies with sales : as entrepreneurs, investors' contributions are appreciated, but what determines a company's value is its current sales and projected profitability in the future; that's what investors look at. In other words, you need customers.

Other countries have a well-established policy of supporting the national economic fabric through public procurement, in particular to encourage the emergence of innovative players. The most obvious example is the United States, where DARPA and BARDA play a central role in pre-ordering from innovative companies. Similarly, NASA bought orbiting services from SpaceX - above the market price - for 11 billion dollars, in order to strengthen this company's competitive position, as part of a very clear strategy whose ultimate aim is to drive [Arianespace] out of the global launcher market. In France, public orders will be worth 111 billion dollars by 2020. Unfortunately, this strategic economic policy tool, essential to the emergence of innovative players, is used very little. In some countries, public procurement is insufficiently geared towards innovative solutions and small businesses. Almost by reflex, public purchasers tend to give preference to large groups when it comes to public procurement contracts, giving them an advantage over smaller, emerging players. Generally speaking, access to public procurement remains extremely complex for innovative SMEs. Wandercraft, for example, took eight years to make contact with the French Ministry of Health. What's more, the exoskeletons acquired by non-profit private mutual hospitals and university hospital centers were not purchased out of their own funds, but through regional and association funds. In 2018, certain regulatory authorities adopted an experimental measure relating to public procurement consisting of opening up to public purchasers the possibility of awarding a public contract without prior advertising or competitive bidding for innovative works, supplies or services and meeting a need with an estimated value of less than $100,000 excluding tax. This measure is interesting, but the threshold set, while undoubtedly suitable for the acquisition of software or digital services, is too low for the purchase of industrial products. What's more, according to a survey by the Economic Observatory of Public Procurement in France, while 72% of public purchasers claim to be aware of this scheme, only 26% say they intend to use it. This discrepancy raises the question of training and raising awareness among public sector players. Ultimately, innovative purchasing only accounts for around 10% of public procurement.

This brings us to the legal and cultural foundations of the primacy of competition. In French law, the primacy of competition defines the fundamental principles of public procurement, with the aim of combating corruption. The result is a hierarchy of texts in favor of competition, to the detriment of support for other public policies. Contrary to certain preconceived ideas, it would be inaccurate to blame European law for the rigidities of French law, since the predominance of competition in French law predates the construction of Europe, and is more marked than in European law, which leaves considerable room for manoeuvre for member states. Germany, for example, has opted not to put its concessions out to tender, and its law on restrictions on competition encourages support for small and medium-sized businesses and innovation, particularly in the social and environmental sectors.

On the contrary, the legal culture of certain countries would lead to a narrow conception of the general principles of public procurement, focused on a normative and legal dimension, to the detriment of economic and social objectives. The resulting rigidity prevents other general interest objectives from being taken into account, both by contracting entities and contracting authorities, and by the administrative courts. Another explanation put forward for the limited use of public procurement to support innovation concerns the risk run by purchasers. Not only do they lack a culture of risk management, but they also run a criminal risk when awarding contracts, through the offences of illegal interest-taking, corruption and, above all, favoritism. In order to be constituted, the latter offence must be based on the intentionality of the perpetrator. In practice, however, judges interpret the offence in almost material terms.

In such legal configurations, we need to make public procurement a major axis of public support for innovation. It is recommended that we revisit our conception of public procurement to consider it as an essential lever of innovation support policy. The first of these levers is to use all the flexibility of the public procurement code to support innovative companies. A precise description of the requirement enables suppliers to be chosen over others, thus favoring innovative French companies. In their invitations to tender, German public purchasers frequently refer, in a perfectly legal manner, to technical standards defined by the German Standards Institute, in order to favor their country's SMEs. Such a practice could easily be replicated in other countries.

In addition, in the defense and security sector, the rules governing public procurement have been made more flexible, in order to extend the possibility of using the negotiated procedure without prior advertising or competitive bidding. In addition, the public purchaser can take account of the need for security of supply and information when choosing a service provider. These options must be fully exploited. Lastly, the innovative purchasing option, already developed in some countries, makes it possible to award public contracts without prior advertising or competitive bidding, up to a limit of $100,000. When this ceiling is not exceeded, this procedure should be used whenever possible.

It is thus possible to favor certain solutions by precisely drafting the call for tenders: It does not appear that public procurement regulations represent a barrier to the development of public purchasing of solutions overall. In fact, public purchasers are encouraged to take into account in their contracts the ways in which they can reduce strategic dependencies, notably by defining their needs and the selection and award criteria. Thus, both through the definition of needs in all public procurement contracts, and through the specific procedures for defense contracts and innovative purchasing, we recommend that maximum use be made of the possibilities offered by existing law to favor local innovative companies, particularly start- ups and SMEs. This strategy implies a profound change in our relationship with the law: we must remain faithful to the fundamentals, and cease to consider that, in the absence of any explicit reference in the Code to a particular practice, it is prohibited.

We must therefore make full use of the flexibility of the public procurement code to encourage innovative companies, and be less cautious in our interpretation of public procurement rules. When two objectives of general interest come into competition, the judge arbitrates between these two requirements by resorting to the notion of proportionality. Following Germany's example, the fundamental principles of public procurement should be enriched to include, alongside the principle of competition and at the same level, other principles such as support for innovation or SMEs, or the objective of sustainable development. In this way, respect for competition could be counterbalanced by other economic and social objectives, while respecting the principle of proportionality. This development would also have the added advantage of being fairly consistent with our legal tradition of reconciling principles. In any case, if a legal change is necessary, we need to target the areas likely to give rise to derogations, such as sustainable development or innovation. In addition, the criminal risk needs to be better controlled, as it excessively hampers the dynamism of public procurement. Support for innovation should be included among the general principles of public procurement law, at the same level as the principle of competition.

In some countries, the ceiling on the innovative purchasing scheme is too low to support industrial innovation, whose products far exceed this threshold. There are several options for modifying the scheme. The innovative procurement threshold could be set as a percentage of the local authority's operating expenditure. This is an interesting idea, but it could prove complex to design and, above all, to implement. We therefore need to advocate greater involvement of local authorities, notably through the action of national agencies for territorial cohesion, which, by reinforcing the transformation of local areas, particularly their digital equipment, could at the same time encourage the use of start-ups and local SMEs. It would be interesting to recommend tripling the ceiling.

Although this threshold is undoubtedly still too low to include large industrial demonstrators, it would nonetheless increase the number of projects eligible for this procedure. For larger projects, such as industrial demonstrators or 1:1 scale models, a second, much higher ceiling (in the range of $1-6 million) would be required.

In addition to the legal measures and adjustments suggested above, in order to amplify innovative purchasing and make it more commonplace, we need to make buyers more aware of the issue, by teaching them about risk. We need to introduce a culture of risk-taking within contracting authorities and entities, to encourage buyers to exploit all the resources of public procurement law, and to dare to select the most competent bidders, even if they are emerging players. It's this change of mentality that certain Defense Innovation Agencies are trying to encourage in certain procurement departments of the Defence Procurement Agency. Albert Einstein said that he who has never failed has never tried, so it's normal, but it's not desirable. We must insist on the need for buyers to learn to take risks, while respecting the rules of public procurement. However, such a development cannot be left to the initiative of purchasing staff alone, and requires impetus and support from the hierarchy. Generally speaking, the purchasing dynamic needs to be more agile.

The more precise and characterized public procurement contracts are, the more we encourage incremental innovation. We make sure that the result in 2026 is what we wanted in 2023, but the world will have changed three times in the meantime, and we run the risk of missing out. The rigidity of public purchasing procedures in some advanced economies can be explained by the fact that the administration's needs when awarding contracts are not sufficiently formulated in concrete requests. In Anglo-Saxon countries, when the public authority places an order, it asks a very concrete question (here's my problem, how can you solve it?). This approach would have been particularly useful in the search for vaccines. In his opinion, such a method would enable us to better target emerging companies and encourage innovation. Finally, to prevent the choice of a solution that turns out to be unsuitable after the fact from putting contracting authorities or entities at risk in future calls for tender, some speakers suggested setting up a guarantee fund to cover public purchasers in the event of difficulties arising from the choice of an innovative solution.

We need to be convinced of the need to adopt, on the scale of other advanced economies, a form of small business act based on the American model. By reserving a portion of public procurement to national economic players other than the major groups, such legislation would help to support the local economic fabric, particularly in terms of innovation. Regulation is undoubtedly less effective than the normal functioning of the market, but, as has been pointed out, the spontaneous inclination of buyers towards established players undoubtedly requires some form of coercion. Some regions have already taken this approach. Some have adopted a public procurement assistance document (guide or charter) with this aim. These documents are designed to help contracting authorities and entities to support the local economic fabric, in full compliance with the public procurement code. In other regions, in partnership with chambers of commerce and industry and local authorities - which are themselves heavily involved in raising awareness of this issue among local authorities - a series of training courses have been designed for buyers, to support them in their efforts.

At community level, it would be appropriate for member states to favor innovative companies in their public procurement, and even, insofar as this is compatible with their public finances, to agree to overpay for their services in order to support their development. However, there is still a long way to go, as illustrated by the German government's space launcher policy: it put Arianespace in competition with the world's other launcher manufacturers to send its satellites into space, and ultimately chose SpaceX as its service provider. This also promotes innovation partnerships. An innovation partnership is a contract for the research and development of innovative products, services or work, and the subsequent acquisition of the resulting products, services or work to meet a need that cannot be satisfied by the acquisition of products, services or work already available on the market. This tool is designed to remedy the difficulties posed by the previous system of pre-commercial procurement and the research and development contract, which required two calls for competition, one for the research and development phase and the other for the acquisition of the solution. The innovation partnership is an integrated system, covering both the research and development phase and the final acquisition of the product, with a single competitive bidding process and the possibility of contracting with several companies in parallel.

Despite the advantages of this system for both public purchasers and innovative companies, few partnerships of this type have yet been concluded. It would therefore be advisable not only to make public purchasers more aware of this option, but also to study the reasons for this low take-up, and consider adapting the system. We also need to take into account the specificities of supporting innovation in the healthcare sector. The healthcare sector is special: as in other fields, start-ups benefit from upstream support from the public authorities, but in the healthcare sector of several countries, there is only one client: the social security system. If they can't talk to this customer and launch projects with him, nothing is possible. The question of reimbursement for innovative drugs and medical devices, and therefore the involvement of the health insurance system, is therefore of paramount importance. This is why it is necessary to ensure that the national health insurance spending target in these countries is defined in such a way as to enable the financing of innovative, potentially costly products: to develop, innovation needs to be rapidly integrated into public health strategies. In this respect, innovation in the healthcare sector should benefit from the creation of Health Innovation Agencies. These agencies will have three objectives: to define a global strategy and ensure its implementation; to simplify existing processes; and to provide support for innovation promoters.

We also need to highlight the difficulty that government departments and public bodies have in understanding the constraints faced by companies, and the handicap that administrative procedures can represent for them. We should also stress the lack of technical, scientific and industrial culture within the administration, with the exception of the Directorate General of Armaments in some countries. The progressive loss of influence of the Ministry of Industry, culminating in its dilution into the Ministry of Economy and Finance, via the creation of a simple Directorate General for Enterprise (DGE), has been accompanied by a loss of skills. For countries with a DGE, the DGE lacks the intellectual wealth and potential of the DGA. These countries will need a Directorate General for Industry or a DGE with the same human resources and capacity for intervention. There's a lot of goodwill out there, but without the skills and resources, there's little chance that we'll succeed in creating powerful industries. In this respect, we should be concerned about the reform of the senior civil service in other countries, which is likely to lead to the abolition of the State's technical corps: we would therefore have profiles with a wider cultural diversity, but fewer people who are highly specialized in certain fields, which is what we need.

This loss of skills has repercussions on the effectiveness of the policy of support for innovative industries. The expert committees convened to select bids are not always equal to the industrial stakes: the process is too light, due to a lack of technical expertise. Even the funding teams seem to be affected by the lack of industrial expertise. The need for technical skills to analyze and support investments must be stressed. According to ExpertActions Group, the people who should be recruited should have this triple skill set: they are highly technical - they are either engineers, doctors or pharmacists - they have almost systematically come from industry or have worked in start-ups, and they have worked in investment. Such skills are essential to be able to critically examine a roadmap and carry out a risk analysis. However, industrial project finance teams are composed exclusively of generalists. This raises the question of whether their investments will have the same relevance and benefit from the same quality of follow-up as those of private funds with multidisciplinary profiles. The lack of in-house technical skills also means that private experts have to be called in to analyze the dossiers of companies applying for public support, which can put them in a tricky situation with regard to business secrecy. To obtain any assistance, they have to reveal their projects to the experts, who come from the competition, exposing them to their direct competitors, which is not possible.

Expertctions Group is concerned about the time it takes to set up an industrial site in certain countries, compared with those of its competitors, due to the length of administrative procedures, particularly environmental ones. Similarly, the risk of litigation against building permits is cited by manufacturers as an impediment to setting up in these countries, due to the long delays involved. The healthcare technology sector, which accounts for 40% of investment in innovative technologies in these countries, seems particularly affected by administrative delays, as illustrated by this example of a vaccine project: the study phase was completed in England before it was launched in France! This is a huge problem.

For any company, time is money, and for a company with no revenues, and therefore no profits, the time constraint is even greater. Authorization procedures for the reimbursement of an innovative drug or medical device also drag on in these countries. The challenge is to integrate innovation quickly and flexibly. The role of the State, in this case, is to do no harm. This means speeding up authorizations and, in the case of healthcare innovations, access to reimbursement, which is the sinews of war. On this last point, there is still work to be done, even if much has been achieved. In some countries, it used to take four to five years to obtain health insurance approval for reimbursement of a drug or medical device, compared with four to six months in Germany! The sequential, rather than parallel, organization of the administrative steps required to validate the launch of an applied research activity is one of the reasons for the longer lead times. A comparison of the authorization stages for a gene therapy laboratory in France and Switzerland shows that a laboratory based in Switzerland starts up its activity nine and a half months before its competitor based in France, mainly due to the simultaneity of the various authorization procedures set up by the Swiss authorities.

We have already highlighted the gap between the time horizons of public research laboratories and companies. This also applies to innovation support schemes, whether at the design stage: it is regrettable that government support plans take several years to be completed, whereas fund-raising takes 18 months. Anything longer than six months poses a problem; when it comes to disbursing aid, players are continually faced with a lack of responsiveness, or even incomprehension. For example, after four months, the funds have still not been received and recruitment is still impossible. But a start-up has no time to lose. In the beginning, they live on funds, but that's not possible forever. Competition is fierce. The slower pace is completely out of step with needs. This is not due to ill will on the part of the administrative or scientific management, but to a lack of knowledge of the industrial environment. Researchers would benefit from a more precise understanding of the constraints of industrialization and the regulatory constraints specific to each field.

Many positive developments have taken place in this area in recent years in several countries. These should be continued and expanded. We would like to highlight the efforts made by administrative authorities to shorten processing times. Some of them are pleased to report that they are meeting their regulatory targets for processing times. In particular, they have achieved this by being more rigorous in their dealings with companies, who used to take advantage of the slowness of the investigation: in the event of an unfavorable conclusion, they would provide additional data, and the products would remain on the market until the Agencies had reached a new decision. As a result, the workings of the committees for the protection of individuals have improved considerably, particularly for level 1 and 2 research involving the human body, which concerns drugs and medical devices. Moreover, a regulation now stipulates that in the event of failure to respond within a certain timeframe, the response is deemed to be positive. What's more, the national agencies for drug and health product safety issue an overall opinion, both regulatory and ethical, on the authorization of the trial, which ensures that the process is well synchronized.

In addition, the introduction of temporary use authorizations has been welcomed, as it allows, under certain conditions, the use and reimbursement of drugs that have not received marketing authorization. However, these mechanisms are of limited use, and do not resolve the issue of delays in the authorization and reimbursement of drugs or devices that do not fall within their scope. Similarly, while some countries have welcomed the introduction of the social security financing law, which enables them to experiment with new healthcare organizations based on novel financing methods, its limitations must also be emphasized. In particular, project sponsors deplore the complexity and length of the procedures involved. We therefore need to considerably shorten processing times under ordinary law, in order to limit the unfavorable comparison with certain countries in this area. In this respect, it is desirable to reduce the time required for administrative procedures, by setting quantified targets. As mentioned above, some countries do not stand out for the simplicity of their systems: many players and contacts are involved. It was this observation that led to the creation of the Health innovation agencies, which will be able to centralize and parallelize requests. This will also help to avoid a number of cumbersome procedures, linked, for example, to the fact that several interlocutors ask the same questions.

The other area for improvement is the engaging dimension of agency responses, as is the case with the US Food and Drug Administration. This authority provides a list of the errands companies have to do to get from one stage to the next, which is very valuable. As a result, a US scientific or regulatory opinion can be used against investors in the event of due diligence. In fact, once a candidate has taken the necessary steps to validate a stage, he or she can be sure that the stage has been reached. The result is greater efficiency and security. We therefore need to systematize the practice of parallel procedures, and require administrations to be bound by their previous responses.

One of the difficulties raised by entrepreneurs is the scarcity of land for business purposes. It is becoming increasingly difficult to find sufficiently large areas available for industrial development. This difficulty is exacerbated by the goal of zero net artificialization of land by 2050, which, however legitimate, inevitably leads to competition in land use. Land is just as important as financing, because it is an element of risk, and therefore an obstacle to financing. If we de-risk the issues, the money will come. This is a question of both regulations and organization between the State and local authorities. A number of initiatives have been taken to remedy this difficulty and make it easier for industries to locate here. In some countries, for example, local authorities have created the Territories of industry scheme, one of whose four priorities is precisely industrial development and land management, with the development of industrial estates and the construction of industrial real estate. This establishment develops solutions to enable manufacturers to save capital and concentrate their resources on production, using, where possible, factory compaction to save surface area. Of course, this initiative also involves local authorities, in particular public establishments for inter-municipal cooperation, which have control over land. The agencies, which are extending their activities beyond the digital sector to support industrial start-ups, are also involved in the project.

The regions are also heavily involved in the search for land for companies. It is essential to be able to offer these companies an adapted land path. An industrial start-up goes through several phases of growth: it may need one or two hectares at the outset, and then have an option to purchase a ten-hectare plot in order to scale up, while freeing up the hectares of the first phase for another industrial start-up. To make it easier to set up industrial facilities locally, we need to strengthen and extend the "urban free zones-entrepreneurial territory" scheme. The aim is to create genuine industrial free zones, along the lines of the existing commercial zones. This system of tax and/or social security exemptions would help boost the country's industrialization. We should build on the turnkey industrial site labeling process, which has so far identified hundreds of sites in certain countries. This system is rightly the cornerstone of government policy to simplify and accelerate the establishment of business activities, as investors must be able to rely on it without encountering any hidden delays following their decision to set up. Nevertheless, we must warn against any deterioration in the quality of the label, which must remain reliable if it is not to undermine investor confidence.

We also urge the executive to map available land and plan its use, in order to respond effectively to companies' needs, and to improve the visibility of available productive land. This requires, in particular, the inclusion of the regions and intercommunal bodies in the process, so as to encourage them to respond to a call for "large site" proposals, making it possible to identify possible locations. Finally, he stresses the absolute necessity, in the context of a scarcity of productive land, of increasing the number of operations to recycle industrial sites. Increase the number of turnkey industrial sites by better planning their use, in collaboration with local and regional authorities, and by giving priority to industrial site recycling operations.

It's also worth noting that one of the reasons why innovative companies relocate to the United States, apart from the fact that the country's private financing is more dynamic, is to gain access to a vast, unified market: same language, same rules (or thereabouts), total freedom of movement for goods, people and capital. At a time when economic and technological developments are accelerating, and the first-mover advantage is becoming ever greater, the challenge of deepening the single market and harmonizing procedures on a regional scale is becoming ever more crucial. The need to obtain authorizations in several countries, difficulties in applying the principle of mutual recognition (which is not an absolute principle), problems linked to the equivalence of tests and certificates in the absence of a common frame of reference, problems linked to labels, the need for translations, administrative costs, additional translations or certificates, etc. are all obstacles that discourage investors and prevent the creation and development of companies. It should be added that one of the priorities is to establish an economy at the service of people by creating more attractive investment conditions and growth that creates quality jobs, particularly for young people and small businesses in a deeper and fairer internal market.

However, while solutions do exist to create a truly single market in certain regions, it has to be admitted that it would be difficult to obtain the necessary agreement and collaboration from the States. In effect, the multiple national authorizations could be replaced by a single authorization valid for all, granted by the national authorities in collaboration at regional level, with fixed administrative costs per category, and the establishment of a common reference system for tests and certificates, resulting in automatic mutual recognition, the use, approved by the competent national authorities, of a digital code by means of which the purchaser could, via his cell phone, find all the information relating to the labels and composition of the product in his national language, but these solutions require the consent and close cooperation of the States and a very high level of digitization of society. Consequently, in view of the handicap represented by the absence of a vast unified market, and despite the challenge that such a development represents, the objective of increasing European integration must be pursued with constancy and diligence. This longer-term objective, which does not depend solely on individual countries, must remain in our sights, as its realization will have a powerful impact on the dynamism of our industry.

In addition, tax incentives need to be redirected, with constant resources. The main tax incentives for innovation are the research tax credit (research tax credit - RTC) and the innovation tax credit (research tax credit - RTC), which have similar mechanisms but different bases. The research tax credit (research tax credit - RTC) is a tax credit that can be deducted from corporate or income tax. It is based on research and development expenditure, and its rate is 30% on average up to $100 million, and 5% thereafter, with no limit on the amount in certain countries. It is described in article 244 quater B of the French General Tax Code. In some countries, the innovation tax credit (CII) system has been modelled on the CIR system, and is governed by the same article of the French General Tax Code. It targets innovation expenditure (design of prototypes and pilot installations for new products), and has an average rate of 20%, with an average ceiling of $400,000 per year. However, unlike the CIR, this tax credit is targeted at SMEs (fewer than 250 employees, sales of less than $50 million or balance sheet total of less than $43 million on average, and not owned by a large group. It is therefore designed to encourage the industrialization of innovative solutions by SMEs.

In most countries undergoing reindustrialization, support for innovation is provided mainly by the research tax credit. In 2020, this tax expenditure, involving some 21,000 companies on average, accounted for 86% of all tax incentives for innovation, and around two-thirds (versus 16.5% in 2000) of total public spending on innovation in the countries concerned. This trend can be partly explained by the quest for neutrality in public aid, to ensure that it complies with State aid rules, but the preference for tax incentives is also linked to the desire not to steer innovation, so as to let the market decide. Most developed countries have introduced tax mechanisms comparable to the CIR; in 2017, 30 of the 35 OECD countries had such a mechanism, as did a number of non-OECD countries, including China. Nevertheless, France remains the country with the most generous tax incentives for innovation.

Despite its high cost to the public purse, the RTC's effectiveness is relatively limited. Its knock-on effect is around 1, on average: the CIR leads companies to increase their internal R&D expenditure by the amount of the CIR received. There is therefore no windfall effect; the impact on R&D spending is real. However, this average masks significant disparities between small companies (for which the knock-on effect is estimated at around 1.4) and large companies (for which it is 0.4, demonstrating the existence of a partial deadweight loss effect). Similarly, the positive effects of the RTC on innovation variables (number of engineers in the workforce or number of patent applications filed) and activity variables (investment or sales) are only observed for SMEs. Yet SMEs, which make up 91% of RTC beneficiaries, account for just 32% of the tax credit. Conversely, the top 10% of beneficiaries receive 77% of the total amount of RTC, and the top 100 receive 33%. Studies also show that this scheme has no effect on the location of foreign groups' research activities, although it does appear to have slowed the relocation of local firms' R&D activities.

The total amount of ITC received averaged $200 million in 2020, and concerned more than 8,000 SMEs on average in all countries. Few studies exist on this scheme, but ExpertActions Group has demonstrated a correlation with an increase in employment, sales and the probability of filing patent applications, although the causal relationship between the use of the ITC and these phenomena has not been established. However, there are two limitations to this scheme. Firstly, the ceiling on eligible expenditure is too low. While it is undoubtedly appropriate for certain industries, the cost of a demonstrator in certain sectors, such as energy, is such that the $400,000 ceiling is far exceeded, and the aid becomes marginal in relation to the investment. On the other hand, the fact that only SMEs are targeted (in terms of headcount, sales, balance sheet total and independence) is detrimental to many innovative companies that have recently outgrown the SME stage. The cost of 250e employees is already high and excluding ETIs from the benefit of the CII may discourage them from expanding. What's more, despite their status as ETIs, the CII can provide these companies with significant assistance in industrializing their innovations.

Whatever the imperfections of these tax credits, we must not call them into question, but propose certain modifications to increase their effectiveness. We must insist on the need to target SMEs more closely through the RTC. We must remain sensitive to the need for predictability on the part of innovation players, and this requires fiscal stability. In a country that is quick to vary its tax rules, the RTC represents an island of stability that companies appreciate. That said, RTC rules have remained unchanged for years in some countries, and it could be argued that the generosity of the system was initially justified by the production cost differential between these countries and others. Since then, however, this differential has been partially eliminated, due in particular to the reduction in corporate and production taxes, not to mention the effect of the employment competitiveness tax credit and cuts in social security contributions, which have reduced labor costs.

In order to guarantee a certain degree of stability and maintain the total RTC budget unchanged, but at the same time to direct the CIR more towards companies on which it has a powerful effect, we are proposing two possible changes. The first is to abolish the 5% rate on average above the $100 million ceiling and, at unchanged total cost, to increase the rate below this ceiling by the same amount. According to calculations, abolishing the RTC above the $100 million threshold would result in average savings of $750 million, which would make it possible to finance an increase in the rate while targeting SME spending more effectively. The amount of the UK equivalent of the RTC depends on the ratio between R&D expenditure and company size, in order to better target SMEs and ETIs. The current RTC is too favorable to large companies, which reduces its macroeconomic impact. A second development is envisaged, which could be combined with the first proposal: calculating the tax credit at holding company level for groups using tax consolidation. Indeed, many large companies consolidate their results for the purpose of calculating their overall profit, so that the losses of some subsidiaries offset the positive results of others, resulting in lower overall corporate tax. However, even in this case, the RTC can be calculated at the level of each subsidiary, depending on the company's choice. We therefore need to aim for the same level for both procedures. According to calculations, such a reform could generate average savings of several hundred million dollars a year, which could, again with an unchanged overall budget, finance a corresponding increase in the RTC rate.

In any case, both of these measures would have to be submitted to the experts for approval, to ensure compliance with the state aid regime. However, as this is a simple resizing of the system, rather than its replacement by a completely different one, the legal risk is fairly limited. Abolish the RTC above the $100 million ceiling by reducing the rate from 5% to 0%, and increase the rate below this ceiling accordingly. This would mean calculating the CIR at the holding company level for tax consolidation groups, and increasing the rate below this ceiling accordingly. While innovation support schemes have proved their worth in the digital sector, they now need to be adapted to the constraints of industry. As mentioned above, the CII scheme is still too limited to be fully effective.

The ceiling should be doubled so that it can contribute to financing large demonstrators, which are very costly. The creation of a demonstrator is a key stage in the industrialization process for innovative products. While upstream research is relatively easy to finance, proof-of-concept and industrialization are much more complex. Yet these are strategic stages in the development of an innovation. This measure could be financed by the tax credit savings generated by the proposed CIR reforms. The CII benefits from a derogation from the ban on state aid for aid granted to SMEs in certain cases. This change, insofar as it introduces a difference in treatment depending on the situation, is likely to contravene the limits set by this derogation; it is therefore necessary to ensure that such a measure complies with state aid regulations.

We should also mention the idea of an innovation voucher, inspired by the Walloon technology voucher, intended exclusively for SMEs and dedicated to financing innovation. The use of this envelope would be left to the discretion of the beneficiary company to carry out innovation projects in-house or through external service providers. With an envelope of $120 million and a coupon of $30,000 per SME or start-up, the scheme would reach 4,000 innovative SMEs. This provision could be financed by the tax savings generated by the CIR measures described above. Such a scheme has the advantage of simplicity, and would broaden the pool of innovation aid beneficiaries to include SMEs that are put off by the bureaucracy associated with innovation support schemes.

As a result, technology transfer can be seen as a source of funding for public research. While there are a number of research transfer structures in developed countries, created at different times, they are all based on the belief that technology transfer organizations can finance technology transfer through revenues from public patents. This belief, which remains dominant today, has largely guided the development of the business model for technology transfer accelerator companies (SATTs), created as part of the first future investment program (PIA) to address certain shortcomings in the technology transfer system, in particular the lack of funding for maturation and proof of concept. A ten-year self-financing target was set at the time of their creation, but this has now been reassessed and extended to fifteen years, i.e. 2024, in view of the difficulties they have encountered in achieving this objective. Indeed, since their creation, all SATTs have recorded a loss in operating income, and it is now widely accepted that SATTs will not achieve financial equilibrium within 10 years. Although the logic of self-financing is specific to the network of thirteen SATTs, it is nevertheless expected that revenues from technology transfer will partly finance the economic model of other technology transfer support structures.

For example, the economic model of the Technological Research Institutes (IRT) and the Institutes for Energy Transition (ITE) continues to evolve, and the State contribution, which represented around 50% of their budget when they were created, is gradually decreasing. By 2025, the authorities hope to achieve a three-thirds funding model: one-third from the State, one-third from private members and one-third from intellectual property revenues, European projects or competitive calls for projects. There is no denying the need to criticize the profit rationale that underpins the technology transfer system and the business model of technology transfer accelerator companies. The technology transfer structures created by the PIAs are based on a business model that demands financial autonomy through patent revenues. This system doesn't work, as was obvious from the outset. The government is trying to make up for its shortcomings, but it will remain inadequate as long as the mission of these structures is primarily to ensure their financial profitability, rather than to help public research and start-ups and SMEs.

The illusion that commercialization can be a source of funding has a number of perverse effects. When it comes to intellectual property, the distribution of rights between the various supervisory bodies in joint laboratories remains complex, despite the progress made with the introduction of the single trustee. The partners sometimes have surreal discussions, during which they argue for six months about what will happen the day they win the lottery. The result is unacceptable delays in drawing up patent exploitation contracts, even though the financial stakes are limited. According to the figures, between 2010 and 2020, an average of 4.9 years elapsed between the filing of a patent and the signing of its exploitation contract. Over the same period, exploitation contracts brought in an average of $183 million, while $130 million was spent on intellectual property costs, severely limiting the return on investment of patent valorization strategies.

In terms of innovation, the projects funded by the SATTs are not necessarily the most innovative, given the selection criteria they apply and their demands for short-term profitability: players are asking questions about the selection criteria applied by the SATTs, which are looking for a short return on investment of three to five years. However, using the Asirpa method (socio-economic analysis of the impact of public agricultural research), they have studied some fifty results and inventions that have been produced, and realized that most of the innovations that are on the market and have been adopted come from long-term research collaborations. Between the start of the research collaboration and the impact on society, it takes ten to fifteen years. They work over a very long time, much longer than in the digital sector. This does not correspond to the SATT criteria.

The need for SATTs to be economically profitable means that they can offer innovative start-ups two models for remunerating technology transfer: either an initial commission followed by royalties directly proportional to the sales generated by the technology transfer; or a hybrid model consisting of an initial commission converted into an equity stake in the company and royalties. However, while these financial structures are acceptable for established companies, they can penalize the development of start-ups. Sales are a key factor in deciding whether or not to invest in a company. As a result, a company that has just been set up is obviously unable to ensure the profitability of a SATT, even though the SATT's KPI (key performance indicator) is based on this perspective. A start-up entrepreneur doesn't want to have 5% of his sales cut!

Similarly, SATTs' demand for fees convertible into equity shares may dissuade investors from acquiring a stake in the start-up, since the company's value-added prospects will be diminished by the SATT's claim on the start-up. SATTs often justify the amount of the up-front fee by the cost of maturation and IP. This practice may give the illusion of an objective value for this amount, but it is not economically sound: if we are looking for reimbursement, why should we be interested only in maturation and IP expenses, and not in the costs of the research that gave rise to the technology? SATTs need to engage in a dialogue with the company on its business plan and on the value actually contributed by the IP transferred, and not, for the sake of convenience, in an approach based on reimbursing expenses.

In addition, universities - particularly the most research-intensive ones, and those that have developed their own commercialization centers - remain fairly critical of the principle of commercialization structures created outside their perimeter, insofar as the SATT business model penalizes them. In fact, the revenues they recover from start-ups as part of their value-added activities enable them to hire new PhD students and carry out resourcing activities. However, until the SATT has recovered all the direct and indirect costs it has incurred in the maturation process, the distribution of revenues between the SATT and the research organization whose research laboratory is at the origin of the technology transfer is very unequal: 35% for the laboratory and 65% for the SATT, for example. As a result, the return on investment for the laboratories behind the technology transfer is delayed.

On the whole, the business model and profitability requirements set for the main research valorization schemes tend to discourage risk-taking, dissuade entrepreneurs from using these structures, and favor investment in projects with short- or medium-term profitability prospects. As a result, there is insufficient investment in technological breakthrough projects with an industrial dimension, as their profitability prospects are not only more distant, but also more uncertain, despite the fact that it is these projects that will enable these countries to become leaders in innovation, and which will provide the most jobs in our territories. A paradigm shift is therefore essential when it comes to implementing measures to support the valorization of research, which should no longer be seen as a means of supporting public research in the short term, or as a source of revenue that is uncorrelated with companies' time, but rather as a long-term investment policy. Transfer and innovation policy must first and foremost be seen as a public investment in the same way as research. It will cost the public establishments that implement it; it's an expense, not a revenue item. To initiate this paradigm shift, we need to propose a radical measure: modify the SATT business model and abandon the chimera of profitability, so as to enable them to better accomplish their maturation policy.

If transfer and innovation policy is an investment, then to be successful it must be the subject of multi-year planning designed to define priorities, guarantee stability in the choices made and provide visibility for researchers, entrepreneurs and investors. We have also discussed the long-term nature of fundamental research, breakthrough technological innovation, industrial profitability and government support. These "long times" now need to be aligned. At government level, a response to this "need for long timeframes" must be found at budgetary level, with the drafting of a multi-year programming law for innovation, but also when examining the programming law for research. It has already been pointed out that the research programming law (LPR) is not clearly linked to the stimulus plan and the future investment plan, even though the amounts involved are considerable. Today, credits allocated to innovation policies are more dispersed than ever, appearing in various budgetary texts, with no real visibility, making parliamentary control work all the more difficult. Although such an approach has begun to be taken, in order to facilitate the coherent management, allocation and steering of resources to support investment in innovation and industry, it is only a partial one, and only a multi-year innovation programming law will make it possible to ensure a comprehensive, clear and coherent approach to budget planning.

This paradigm shift also implies the adoption of a systematic assessment of the economic and social impact of research projects that are subject to commercialization. Indeed, the evaluation criteria used - primarily revenues from research commercialization - do not allow for a fair, effective and sovereign approach to technology transfer policies. Technology transfer and innovation policy is not seen as primarily aiming for economic impact, but as a source of research funding. It includes two indicators: the impact of the research tax credit (CIR) and the financing of public operators by the private sector. That says it all. More precisely, the second objective, to promote transfer and innovation, includes only these two indicators, whereas a logic more geared towards the socio-economic evaluation of transfer and commercialization policies would suggest setting other criteria, for example : the number of companies created, which would make it possible to value the creation of start-ups as a means of organizing innovation transfers; the number of direct and indirect jobs created, which would make it possible to assess the effects of valorisation policies on national employment; changes in the sales and employment figures of start-ups five years after their creation, in order to check whether the start-ups supported had genuine growth potential; the number of patents actively used, as the criterion of the number of patents filed is insufficient in several respects: a registered patent that is not transferred to a company, that is not economically valorized and that does not ultimately meet a market need is a lost patent; the number of patents resulting from public research that are valorized by local companies, in order to integrate considerations of sovereignty into the evaluation process (indeed, numerous examples have been cited of foreign companies valorizing and benefiting from patents and innovations made possible by the financing and support provided by local public authorities, such as certain drugs developed by Inserm Transfert but marketed by American companies.

Such a change of methodology in the preparation of the budget report would also be consistent with the adoption of a multi-year innovation programming law: the State's stance is that of a long-term investor who evaluates its return on investment for the benefit of the French research and innovation ecosystem. Adopt economic, social and sovereignty criteria to assess the program's objective of promoting transfer and innovation. In addition to being taken into account when drawing up the State budget, this paradigm shift by promoting a culture of economic and social evaluation must also be implemented by and within public research organizations. While some research organizations already carry out such socio-economic assessments internally, they need to be strengthened, their data aggregated at a macroeconomic level, and these assessments made systematic. Evaluation can also be based on the alignment of transfer policies with the political priorities set for innovation and research, along the lines of the method for socio- economic analysis of the impacts of public agricultural research, which takes into account, for example, the effects of innovations on the environment, the ecological transition in agriculture being one of the major political priorities for the coming years. We need to emphasize the need to strengthen the ex-post evaluation of transfer and commercialization policies.

Existing public financing, support and assistance schemes are not always well suited to the specific needs of innovative industrial companies. Firstly, the duration of financial support, short- or medium-term profitability requirements, low risk appetite and lack of knowledge of industrial issues do not allow us to adapt to the duration inherent in the development of certain innovations. For example, it takes a minimum of ten to fifteen years to develop a drug, seven to nine years for a medical device, and five to seven years for digital health innovations. In other words, the drugs coming out today were developed over fifteen years ago. Secondly, the development of innovative companies with an industrial vocation is capital- intensive, requiring substantial investment right from the early stages of development, not least because of the infrastructures to be financed. In France, significant efforts have been made by the public authorities to develop seed funding, and private investment has taken over from this. However, the volume of financing granted remains lower than in other European countries, and insufficient to finance industrial-scale projects. According to the venture capital barometer drawn up by the consultancy firm Ernst & Young, the average amount raised in France in 2021 was $14.76 million, compared with several tens of millions of dollars in countries such as the UK and Germany.

In addition, there is a lack of growth funds capable of financing industrial innovations to the tune of several tens of millions of dollars, and especially of raising capital in excess of $100 million. Thirdly, the development of industrial and technological innovations involves specific, ongoing risks: projects need to be supported over very long periods. The phases follow one another: risk linked to the technology used, then risk linked to the product, then problems of industrialization, commercialization and marketing. Last but not least, the development of an industrial innovation over several years also represents a challenge in terms of human resources, not only for the teams of researchers in charge of development, but also for investors and investment funds, who need to recruit profiles with an awareness of industrial issues.

In view of the specificities and difficulties inherent in the development of industrial innovations, it would appear that the financing continuum of the ecosystem in certain countries has gaps that can be detrimental, as the profits from French patents, inventions and innovations benefit foreign companies capable of mobilizing massive amounts of capital to commercialize and develop them on a larger scale. On the one hand, from the point of view of company start-ups, while the amounts raised are significant at an aggregate level, they remain limited at the level of individual companies. For example, over the past few years, it is estimated that seed funding has been working fairly well, but seed funds do not have the same capacity as other ecosystems, as Biotech's A rounds represent a few million, whereas in the UK or Germany, we're talking about 10 to 20 million. This company doesn't have enough seed funds specialized in HealthTech, particularly in biotech in France.

On the other hand, at the growth fund stage, there is a risk that local companies, whose creation and start-up have been financed by local investors and whose innovations are sometimes the result of public research, will be bought out by foreign investors, who will reap the benefits of commercialization and hence the return on investment. These risks are all the greater in the case of companies with an industrial vocation. In fact, if foreign investment funds finance the development of innovations resulting from local research during the growth and industrialization phases, there is a risk that the company will be set up abroad rather than locally. Finally, at the IPO stage, it is vital to ensure the final link in the financing chain, i.e. the listing of innovative companies, in particular by enabling local unicorns to be listed and obtain financing from stock market systems: this is the aim of the Tech Leaders initiative set up this year by Euronext. However, the American Nasdaq is still considered more prestigious and more successful. Few local companies are listed on Nasdaq. There are a few dual listings. On the other hand, listing on Nasdaq is the goal of many entrepreneurs.

In addition to the initiatives taken by public authorities to support the development of industrial and deep-tech start-ups, for which an average budget of 2.3 billion dollars is allocated, several initiatives and adaptations are required on the private investment side. Firstly, local funds, particularly those involved in the start-up and seed stages, need to step up their skills to adapt the financing ecosystem to industrial, scientific and technological challenges. Indeed, investment fund teams are not always equipped with sector-specific knowledge, and the technical component of a financing application is often underestimated in favor of its financial component: financing industrial acceleration is not just a problem for investors with a financial profile (it's not enough to know how to manipulate Excel). To scale up a factory, you need to invest tens and tens of millions of dollars: you need to understand which machines to buy, how much it will cost, and so on. And, if you don't understand the underlying technology, you can't make the right judgment).

As a result, it is important to encourage high-level, multi-disciplinary teams within investment funds, whether in the public sector or private companies, in order to cross-fertilize financial, scientific, technological and industrial expertise, which presupposes diversifying recruitment, for example by hiring PhD students in life sciences or engineers. Supporting the creation of seed funds specializing in disruptive technologies, industry and biotechnologies, through the introduction of multi-disciplinary curricula and dual curricula in the training of financial analysts, would be one way forward. It has to be said that adapting the start-up financing ecosystem to industrial challenges also means decentralizing funding. Indeed, 82% of financing is still concentrated in national capitals, while 50% of start-ups are created outside them. Digital start-ups, on the other hand, are mainly based in major cities, as are investment funds. We therefore need to encourage their presence within local ecosystems, so that they can discover the industrial start-ups, projects and technological nuggets of the future.

Use territorial networking to attract private financing to industrial start-ups and innovative companies located outside major cities. In addition, several countries could draw more inspiration from Germany, where industrial families, through their asset managers, are increasingly involved in supporting the industrial innovation ecosystem.

According to an analysis by Ernst & Young, family offices are becoming benchmark investors, even though they account for just 2.5% of the global M&A market, and benefit from several advantages: a more flexible investment strategy, sector expertise and longer holding and allocation periods than other funds. Finally, we could consider assigning tax funds - innovation mutual funds (FCPI) and local investment funds (FIP) - a target, in the form of a quota, for investment in innovative industrial companies.

The need to massify growth funds should be highlighted. From now on, we need to increase our capacity to mobilize large amounts of capital. Beware of the culture of "enough is enough": we need to pull out all the stops. This observation is shared by players in the fields of biotechnology, connected medicine, life sciences and therapeutic and medical innovations. From this point of view, even if an ecosystem of private funding is beginning to take shape, several countries are lagging behind. In Belgium, for example, there are already at least two investment funds specializing in the seed stage of biotech therapeutics at over $100 million, whereas there is only one in France. To increase the volume of local growth funds, we need to transform investment in the technology sector with more late-stage and global tech funds, for a total of $20 billion, with a target of ten late-stage funds managing at least $1 billion. With an average of $18 billion already raised by approved funds, including $3.5 billion invested by institutional players, the initial funding target has been raised to $30 billion, testifying to the success of this initiative for digital and technology players.

However, the persistent difficulties encountered by some companies and investment funds in working with institutional players should be highlighted, particularly in the healthcare sector: although funds have been accredited, players are finding it harder to raise funds from institutional investors than they do in the IT sector generally. There are several reasons for this: the life cycle is longer, the capital intensity is higher, and the risk profile is higher. This is why we need to organize training to encourage these investors, the Limited Partners (LPs), to invest in the healthcare sector, and to make them aware of the life cycle of companies and the challenges of healthcare, which seem obvious.

To ensure the final stage in the financing chain for innovative companies, it is essential to have a European ecosystem that is appropriate, large-scale and set up at the right time. Given the growth of technology and digital companies in countries undergoing reindustrialization, and the increasing number of unicorns in this field, the time seems right to create a European stock market ecosystem capable of supporting and listing these companies. There is not necessarily a consensus on the right method to adopt. On the one hand, there are those who consider that the current offer is sufficient, even if there is some mistrust among entrepreneurs and investors linked to IPOs carried out too early in the past by companies that did not yet have the critical mass to finance themselves directly on the financial markets. On the other hand, there are those who consider that the offer is not a credible alternative to listing local technology champions abroad, and that a regional Nasdaq should be created instead.

There are now local digital and technology companies that are sufficiently mature and well-funded upstream to develop a dedicated market offering. However, it is still too early to develop such an offering specifically for industrial start-ups. Indeed, there is a real risk that such companies will turn to the financial markets too early, when there is a prior need to consolidate the previous links in the financing chain, particularly at the level of growth funds: for companies with industrial investments to make, it is more difficult to find an abundance of private equity capital. This is why they turn to the stock market earlier than others, especially if they are in Biotech or Cleantech, even if those in Cleantech can call on a few specialized funds. It therefore seems important to proceed in stages, firstly by complementing the seed phase with funds that are better trained in industrial issues, then by massively increasing growth funds, and finally by creating a specific stock market segment for these companies to enable them to obtain financing at the right moment in their development on the financial markets.

It's worth noting that the relationship between large companies and innovative small businesses, whether start-ups or SMEs, is not uniform: some major groups build and maintain close relationships with a network of small, innovative companies that benefit all stakeholders. For example, the Air Liquide Group has put in place a strategy of active monitoring, support and partnerships with relevant start-ups in its sector. It hosts around ten of them in its start-up deep-tech gas pedal and strives to build lasting relationships with them, based on the development of these young start-ups outside their relationship with Air Liquide. However, we must deplore the deleterious attitude of most major groups towards them. The general feeling can be summed up by the incisive phrase used by one of them: local major groups regard start-ups with indifference, if not contempt.

Moderna's experience is illuminating in this respect. When the company had to industrialize vaccine production at the beginning of 2020, no major pharmaceutical company, either local or foreign, agreed to enter into a partnership of the kind that linked BioNTech to Pfizer in the same field. Furthermore, the commercial relationships forged between large groups and smaller companies are not only governed by excessively complex and detailed general terms and conditions of sale - which can be taken or left - but often boil down to a purely customer-supplier relationship to the advantage of the large group, which can be inflexible towards its suppliers. When a company finds itself in difficulty in supplying one of its key accounts with its product under contractual conditions, due to the rising cost of raw materials, it is told that it has signed a contract and must honor it.

Similarly, major groups tend to pass on to their subcontractors the compensation clause imposed on them in certain contracts, in order to avoid exposing their own technology to competition, thus transferring the risk of know-how plundering and loss of technological lead to SMEs. This attitude is harmful for several reasons. Not only is it detrimental to the vitality and longevity of small industrial companies - SMEs and start-ups - it is also detrimental to the ecosystem in which large groups operate. Indeed, the network of SMEs that gravitate around them is a key element in their competitiveness, and it is in their interest to support and consolidate it, in particular by helping start-ups and SMEs to conquer other markets beyond this ecosystem. Competitiveness clusters were set up to encourage interaction between large corporations, SMEs and start-ups, in order to make this ecosystem more robust, but with little success, according to most speakers. Some SMEs working on collaborative programs with major groups even realized that they were not referenced by these groups, and that they were unable to offer them their services, even though they had worked together! The indifferent, even distrustful attitude of large companies towards smaller ones, especially start-ups, stemmed from a lack of understanding of the latter's business model. The top executives of major French companies are said to lack a start-up culture, and to misunderstand the challenges, constraints and workings of start-ups. This lack of understanding is counter-productive for the ecosystem.

This leads us to ask whether the takeover of a start-up by a major corporation is an opportunity or predation? The subject of the takeover of innovative companies by large corporations is a complex one. For an investor, the prospect of buying out the company in which he has invested, once it has developed, represents an exit horizon. Thus, an economy in which large corporations are on the lookout for innovative companies to acquire is likely to reassure investors and encourage them to finance the start-up or development of innovations carried by small companies. What's more, an innovative company may, at some point in its existence, need a massive and rapid injection of capital and experience to industrialize a solution and bring it to market. Being able to rely on the industrial, financial and commercial clout of a large group can be a real asset.

Last but not least, the acquisition of a start-up by a large group enables the latter to benefit from the start- up's innovative dynamics and agility, and to generate competitive advantages more strongly and rapidly than through in-house R&D alone. On this subject, several speakers, including directors of investment funds specializing in the healthcare sector, deplored the overly wait-and-see attitude of large pharmaceutical companies, who defer buying start-ups until their product has been proven effective, or even until it has been introduced on the market. The start-up and its investors take on the risk alone. A number of speakers expressed concern about the predatory acquisition strategy of certain major groups, aimed at sterilizing innovations that would challenge their dominant position in strategic technology markets. While your information mission is aware that this policy is justified at the microeconomic level by the concern of the major group to cut short the ambitions of certain innovative start-ups and SMEs to dethrone them in their sector of activity, at the macroeconomic level, these predatory acquisitions seriously undermine our economy's ability to transform innovation into economic spin-offs, as well as the renewal of the industrial fabric.

Large local groups need to change the way they look at the innovative companies around them, and move from the role of indifferent or even hostile giant to that of benevolent big brother, as is widely done in other countries (Germany, USA, Japan, etc.). The first lever is innovative purchasing. The speakers we heard criticized public procurement for not supporting innovation enough, but in reality, the purchasing policy of major groups is not much more dynamic. Generally speaking, the purchasing procedures of major accounts are long, complex, rigid and, above all, just as cautious as those of public authorities. Yet Microsoft and Intel first emerged as IBM subcontractors, and Boeing today supports the entire economy of the American aeronautics industry... On a more general note, major corporations would do well to develop a richer relationship with innovative companies than that between customer and supplier.

Some major local groups are already aware of this issue. The aforementioned Air Liquide, for example, does its utmost to maintain a network of dynamic start-ups, and when an acquisition appears to be the only solution for supporting innovation, or when it fits directly into the company's overall strategy, it ensures that the terms of the buyout are balanced and respect the interests of the target company's founders. Indeed, the assets of an innovative start-up are essentially its technical staff, and if they leave the company as a result of a hostile transaction, the acquired company is largely stripped of its substance. The LVMH group was also cited as a group that pays close attention to supporting the ecosystem in which it operates. Its suppliers include the last local SME to master the art of lace-making, and it is careful to anticipate all the company's needs in order to guarantee its survival. Despite these positive examples, many SMEs and start-ups regret the lack of industrial or R&D collaboration with their key accounts. It's important to stress that start-ups and SMEs can benefit from the infrastructures of major groups to industrialize their products. The example of the 3ED Group, which made its production capacities available to a start-up from the School of Arts and Crafts manufacturing exoskeletons during the health crisis, has been highlighted, but it remains an isolated case.

Finally, major groups would do well to reflect on their strategy of investing in start-ups, either to buy them out, or to ensure their development and thus benefit from their technology, thereby strengthening the ecosystem in which they operate: a chain is only as strong as its weakest link. The case of Polymem is representative of this type of virtuous behavior: this company had orders that required doubling its production capacity. It was unable to find an investment fund with the courage to risk an industrial investment. Thanks to its expertise, it benefited from the fact that an American operator in the vaccine production chain needed to ensure the reliability of this essential supplier; it was able to negotiate a strategic partnership with this operator, which bought it out, guaranteeing that its production and research centers would remain with it. Thanks to this partnership, Polymem was able to quadruple its production capacity and set up locally this American company's technical representation and center of expertise for Europe. However, this situation does not eliminate the risk associated with a foreign takeover of an innovative company: access to cutting-edge technology and, potentially, relocation.

Some major local groups have understood the importance of supporting their ecosystem, and to this end have set up support systems and corporate venture funds to invest in start-ups. Renault's strategy is a good illustration of this. Along with five other CAC 40 companies, the group has formed an alliance - Software République - housing an incubator for start-ups active in the mobility sector, which are supported and accompanied by the various members through calls for projects. It has also invested in a $250-300 million fund, launched by a former employee and specializing in the circular economy and sustainable mobility. Finally, it directly supports start-ups in its ecosystem by giving them access to its production lines and placing orders with them to equip certain electric vehicles. These initiatives show that the mindsets of some major companies are moving in the right direction, but this movement needs to accelerate.

Should virtuous behavior be encouraged through corporate social responsibility criteria? Corporate social responsibility (CSR) has been gradually introduced into local law, notably by the law on new economic regulations. It has been modified by several other legislative texts, and is now subject to certification. The texts mainly provide for the publication of extra-financial performance data in seven areas: corporate governance, consumer protection, contribution to local development, human rights, working conditions, environment and good business practices. Including data on partnerships with innovative start-ups and SMEs, whatever their form - innovative purchasing, industrial partnerships, compliance with payment deadlines, research and development collaboration, etc. - in the CSR communication materials of major corporations could provide an incentive for a change in approach. - could be an incentive for major corporations to change their attitudes and practices towards innovative companies. The reputational effect of CSR is a strategic element to which companies attach importance, as it can facilitate or complicate their relations with investors, the regulator, consumers, job applicants, etc. In particular, we need to emphasize the asset that large local groups could represent for the development of innovation, if more of them adopted a policy of support for innovative SMEs. We must therefore advocate a change in the attitudes and practices of large companies towards SMEs in their sector, in order to reinforce the robustness of their ecosystem.

Making industrial property and standardization sources of competitiveness. Intellectual property (IP), and in particular industrial property, is a major source of competitiveness for companies and the economy. Yet this issue is little-known by companies and public authorities alike. Local companies, especially SMEs and ETIs, but also public authorities, have not fully grasped the strategic importance of protecting innovations through IP. A joint study by the European Patent Office (EPO) and the European Union Intellectual Property Office (EUIPO) shows that the sales per employee of IP owners are 20.2% higher than those of non-owners, and that the average salary of their employees is 19.3% higher than that of non-owners. These differences rise to 36.3% and 52.6% respectively for patent holders alone (i.e. excluding trademark and design holders). Finally, if we consider SMEs alone, sales per employee are 68% higher in companies with IP rights than in those without.

It has to be said that IP protection is a powerful competitive factor. Firstly, a patent immediately gives its owner a considerable advantage in the marketplace, both in terms of time - the first innovator on the market takes a dominant position - and money, since competitors will have to spend at least as much as the owner on research and development to come up with a high-performance solution that is sufficiently different from the one protected by the patent. Secondly, the number of patents is, for a company's partners, a good indicator of the innovative nature of its activity, since a patent can only be granted for a new and inventive process or product. In this way, IP signals the effectiveness of the company's industrial strategy. Finally, IP protection is a driving force behind innovation. Indeed, taking steps to protect IP means coming face to face with competitors' patents. In this way, you can either realize that you're reinventing the wheel, or, if you demonstrate real differentiating elements compared with the competition, you can develop these further to increase value gains. Industrial property attorneys (IPAs) work alongside their clients to help them adopt the best IP strategy and best protect their competitive advantages.

Every year, the World Intellectual Property Organization publishes an overview of countries' innovation performance. One of the key indicators is the number of patent applications filed in relation to GDP, in purchasing power parity. In 2021, France, for example, will have 7.5 applications per billion dollars, compared with 15.7 in Germany, a ratio of 1 to 2. What's more, of the 15,000 or so patent applications filed per year locally - a figure that has been stable for the past twenty years - only around 2,500 come from innovative

SMEs, while 20,000 SMEs benefit from the CIR. By comparison, German SMEs and especially ETIs file a very large number of patent applications, since small German applicants (with fewer than 10 filings per year) account for 32% of all filings - around 13,500 - a ratio of 1 to 5. Even within large groups, the materialization of innovation through patents obtained is not as important as might be expected. For example, the French champions in patent filings include companies from the aerospace (Airbus, Safran, Thales) and automotive (Renault, Stellantis, Valeo) sectors, but no French energy or telecoms company. Internationally, 80% of the top 50 companies filing patent applications are in the IT sector. Yet the world's most innovative countries - the United States, Japan, South Korea and China - are also those which file the most international patent applications, whatever the technology. The number of patent applications filed with the European Patent Office by China, for example, rose by 25% between 2020 and 2021.

The public authorities themselves have long neglected this issue, and have not developed a coherent patent policy, particularly with regard to research operators. It was not until the law on research programming that knowledge transfer and its use in all areas contributing to economic, social and cultural progress were recognized as part of the duties of teacher-researchers. It is also this law that requires knowledge transfer activities and their application in business to be taken into account in the evaluation of research staff. In the field, however, attitudes are slow to change. As far as the ability to establish links with the industrial world is concerned, universities have not necessarily integrated the creation of patents or start-ups into the evaluation and promotion of their teaching and research staff. The main indicators are still teaching investment and the number of publications. Things are changing, however, as innovation has become a key issue for universities.

The priority given to publications can not only act as a brake on technology transfer, insofar as it prevents patent applications from being filed, but it can also encourage competitors to freely exploit the published results of our researchers' work. At government level, the PIA has financed the creation of patent structures to support companies in commercializing their innovations. The law has also introduced a series of measures to ensure greater legal certainty for local patent holders. However, these countries do not have a national strategy to support the protection of industrial property (IP), as is the case in other countries. In South Korea, for example, a general secretariat for IP has been set up under the Prime Minister's office. Similarly, when Japan wished to change the scale of patent filings, it set up an IP committee chaired by the Prime Minister. In China, the government has devised a proactive policy to encourage the filing of patent applications at regional level, with financial incentives.

Given the role of intangible assets in a company's competitiveness, it is vital to make local SMEs and ETIs aware of the strategic dimension of IP. The lack of dynamism shown by local companies when it comes to IP protection stems mainly from an underestimation of the economic importance of patents, to such an extent that many of them admit, when applying for innovation aid, that they have no industrial strategy. In order to develop a long-term vision of the subject, public authorities need to engage in a proactive policy in favor of IP protection. Funding agencies have begun to take up the issue, notably through strategic diagnostics of intellectual property and valuation of intangible assets, offered to innovative start-ups, SMEs and ETIs, with 80% of the costs covered. The aim of this tool is to encourage the emergence of a relevant IP strategy within companies, and to enable managers to better assess the value of their intangible assets. This tool is a first step in raising awareness of the importance of industrial property.

It would also be appropriate for the executive to take up this issue at the highest level, in order to design and implement a national strategy in this area. At present, IP issues are divided up between multiple players. This fragmentation prevents the emergence of the overall vision needed to define an IP strategy. The creation of an ad hoc, agile and efficient coordinating body would facilitate the definition of a national industrial property strategy aimed at increasing the number and economic impact of patents held by local innovation players. This body could take the form of a High

Commission for Industrial Property. We also need to advocate the centralization of patent information in order to map patents by technological sector. Active patent data management has a number of benefits: it provides all innovation players (companies, research operators, development organizations, etc.) with a consolidated view of existing patents in their field(s) of activity, and facilitates monitoring work; it facilitates the creation of patent clusters; and it can serve as a basis for setting up alliances between French companies by sector, in order to purchase patents jointly and thus divide costs.

Over the next five years, states are expected to spend an average of $20 billion to support innovation. If, in 2027, the number of patent applications filed is still close to 15,000 per year, we can legitimately wonder whether this sum will really have been invested in innovation. Create a High Commission for Industrial Property to integrate this dimension at the highest level into the overall strategy for supporting innovation. We also need to highlight the fact that local players, both public and private, are not sufficiently involved in regional and international standardization bodies, which are nevertheless a powerful lever for supporting innovation and industry. Indeed, depending on how standards are defined, a particular technology may be favored, and consequently all the industries that have chosen that technology. Some countries, such as Germany, have perfectly understood the importance of active participation in such bodies. Even if a company holding essential standard-related patents (BEN) is obliged to conclude licenses with its competitors on fair, reasonable and non-discriminatory terms, holding such a patent nevertheless represents an advantage for the holder. However, the indifference of certain local players to this activity is detrimental to the interests of our companies.

Chapter 3

Takeover for better local entrepreneurship

> The demographics of business owners are alarming: 25% of managers are over 60, and 11% are over 66 on average. Estimates of the number of businesses to be sold over the next 10 years range from 250,000 to 700,000. In the meantime, governments are communicating more on business start-ups than on business takeovers, even though, in the absence of buyers, the retirement of managers will lead to the disappearance of businesses. The health and economic crisis is also having an impact, making the context even more complex. Many small business owners are inclined to sell up sooner than expected, accelerating the natural process of departures.

In addition, it has weakened the financial position of companies, some of which have become potential targets. The phenomenon of predation is felt more strongly. Takeovers by foreign investors, in the absence of a local buyer, can sometimes prove disastrous, as some buyers quickly relocate the business. Finally, the public debate has evolved, with some positions particularly critical of the current arrangements. They often mix up the assessment of business assets with that of private assets, and fail to take into account the positive externalities of family businesses.

Why is company takeover so essential? Advanced economies need their SMEs to grow into mid-sized companies (MSEs), which are essential to their economic performance, employment and the recovery of their trade balances. Yet, on average, it takes 21 years for a company to become an ETI. Keeping companies in their home regions guarantees their economic vitality and employment. In the absence of a new owner, retirement can lead to the loss of know-how, patents, jobs, competitiveness and, depending on the sector, economic sovereignty. This chapter proposes policies to combat the difficulties of transferring businesses in advanced economies. Relayed on the ground by business leaders and consular chambers, these difficulties are perceived both as a personal tragedy for business leaders of retirement age wishing to find a buyer, but also as a challenge for the territories where these businesses determine their economic vitality and the maintenance of employment. The challenge is not just a local one, since it includes maintaining the know-how that contributes to our competitiveness.

The disappearance of certain companies, for lack of a buyer or due to relocation following a takeover by a foreign investor, can also prove detrimental to our economic sovereignty. The health crisis and supply difficulties have highlighted the problem of economic dependence, as they have heightened awareness of the consequences of the cessation of certain types of production on our territory. The current economic context is also forcing us to take a fresh look at the issue of business transfers. It was with this new perspective, and the realization that the subject of business transfers almost invariably comes up in discussions with business owners, that the idea for the book's chapter was born. The aim is to take stock of the progress made, and formulate policy recommendations. However, despite this modernization of the framework for business transfers, it has to be said that the problem remains. Unfortunately, the players involved have not seen a surge in the field to compensate for the ageing demographic of business leaders. Even more worrying is the recent position of the Economic Analysis Council (CAE) in certain countries, which calls into question the value of family transfers and the economic benefits of such incentives. The CAE suggests that the most appropriate solution would be to drastically reduce or even abolish exemptions in favor of payment facilitation mechanisms. However, both family transfers and the essential nature of the scheme have already been amply demonstrated. This attempt to call the system into question is not insignificant, and deserves to reaffirm the need to secure the Pactes de transmission for future transfers, so that more SMEs can become ETIs and thus contribute to local economic growth.

The proposals presented here are based on two main themes: securing and simplifying. These 11 recommendations also meet 5 priority objectives: to stabilize the current law in response to the main demand from company directors; to safeguard the stock of transferable assets, essential for family transfers and the development of local ETIs; to simplify procedures and mechanisms to facilitate transfers and takeovers; to secure transfers by limiting the destabilizing effects of case law or certain administrative decisions; to encourage directors to anticipate their transfer. It should be remembered that business transfers include both intra-family transfers and transfers to third parties (whether employees or not).

In this respect, it's worth noting a worrying fact about the survival of local businesses. In addition to the 60,000 business transfers per year on average in developed countries, 30,000 businesses disappear. It's worth remembering that the first obstacle to taking better account of the challenge of business transfers is precisely the lack of reliable statistics. As most statistical institutions have stopped counting transfers, the inclusion of transfers is no longer coordinated, and varies according to the criteria used in studies published on the subject. The most reliable figures on transfers are provided by the ExpertActions Group. Their latest studies clearly show that the slowdown in business transfers has become more pronounced: transfer transactions fell by 19% between 2010 and 2019, showing that the idea that the ageing of managers determines the number of transfers is false; the slowdown has, unsurprisingly, been confirmed between 2019 and 2020, with a further fall of 16%. And yet the stakes have never been higher, given the demographics of the management population. What's more, the economic crisis is likely to prompt many business owners to hand over their businesses sooner than expected.

From a demographic point of view, the figures are quite alarming. In 2005, 15% of SME managers were over 60, compared with 25%

today; 5.5% of managers were aged 66 or over, compared with over 11% today. In his contribution, the latter notes that, over a long period, the number of transfers has fallen steadily in recent years, particularly for entities with no employees, while it has been more stable for employing VSEs (1 to 9 employees). At best, the trend is slightly upward for SMEs, but this is out of all proportion to the wave of transfers expected as the baby-boom generation retires. We estimate that, over the next 10 years, an average of around 700,000 companies in advanced economies will potentially find themselves in a situation of divestment. The market is huge, and represents a huge number of jobs. For ExpertActions Group, one out of every two ETIs will be transferred in the next few years. By 2022, the market is estimated to average 80,000 companies, with an average of around 1 million jobs. On average, between 7,000 and 9,000 companies are transferred each year. Generally speaking, transfers are a "blind spot": there's a lot of talk about start-ups, but very little about transfers. This blind spot is indeed striking when we look at the public authorities' support for business start-ups.

Some countries are a little too focused on the idea of creation. This leads to a general fragmentation of the productive fabric and works against the internal growth of companies. At the same time, the number of people taking over existing, profitable businesses is proving insufficient. This observation is shared by ExpertAcions Group, which regrets that company takeovers are not given greater local support, particularly in a context of competition between countries that should, on the contrary, result in sustained efforts to bring more mid-sized companies into being. As a reminder, in 2021, according to ExpertActions Group, the number of business start-ups in advanced economies reached a new record with 995,900 start-ups on average, i.e. 17% more than in 2020, the year of the previous record despite a sharp decline in start-ups during the first confinement in 2020. The number of business creations is thus almost 80% higher than its average level over the period 2010 to 2017, before the recent expansion in the number of business start-ups. This growth was driven by company start-ups (+24%) and sole proprietorships under the micro-entrepreneur scheme (+17%).

For ExpertActions Group, a structural problem we see is a lack of anticipation on the part of sellers. Some companies are sold too late, or not at all, due to a lack of preparation. We need to combat this lack of anticipation. There is indeed a paradox when we look at the age of managers on the one hand, and sales on the other. It can be illustrated by the phrase "intention is not disposal".

In fact, cross-referencing data on completed sales, i.e. sales actually carried out, with data from a survey of managers to ascertain their desire to sell, reveals that intentions to sell are naturally more frequent among older managers, but that they are only very partially transformed into sales. It appears that less than half of these intentions are transformed into sales when the manager is over 60, whereas this difference is insignificant when the manager is under 55. There are many reasons for this: unpreparedness on the part of the manager, management of day-to-day business taking up too much energy, reserve price of the sale too high for potential buyers, difficulties in finding a buyer they can trust, limited appeal on the part of buyers for certain types of activity or company location... It's also worth remembering that only 17% of VSE managers manage to sell their business after the age of 65.

On a macroeconomic level, we need to describe more precisely the risk inherent in the difficulties of transferring ownership and the ageing of company directors: a director who wishes to sell tends to lose debt and disinvest. If this period lasts a year or two, the consequences for the company are not too serious. However, given the great difficulty older managers have in selling, this period can sometimes last up to 10 years. During this long period, when a business owner is not investing or developing new projects, the company loses value and becomes less and less saleable. The likelihood of selling is therefore reduced. Given that 25% of SME managers are over 60, this practice is spreading to an increasingly large proportion of the local SME fabric, which tends to weigh on the overall investment rate of SMEs. There is also the danger of a gradual reduction in a company's growth potential.

Studies show that the phenomenon of ageing business leaders is very noticeable at local level. The proportion of managers over 65 is particularly high in three areas. Firstly, it clearly highlights what some geographers call the "diagonal of emptiness", an area of low density and demographic decline. It is also particularly marked in industrial zones. Conversely, in the reference ecosystems for medium-sized companies and ETIs, and in most of the zones of influence of metropolises, this phenomenon is much less marked. However, the distribution of this single age variable conceals the heterogeneity of territorial situations in terms of renewal of the business fabric at the end of professional activity. A typology exercise that takes into account not only the age structure, but also the rate of ageing and the frequency of transfers and disappearances, particularly after the age of 60, reveals groups of territories ranked in descending order of fragility.

Group A brings together the regions where the situation is most critical, with the proportion of managers aged over 65 exceeding 12% and growing at a worrying rate, despite the already high rates of transfer and family transmission. In Group B, the ageing trend is less marked, but is becoming more pronounced as a result of a very low transfer rate. To halt the deterioration in these areas, which are at the threshold of the previous group, a rapid and significant upturn in the takeover of SMEs at the end of their professional activity is therefore necessary, unless we accept a gradual devitalization of the local productive fabric. Group C is slightly less worrying in terms of age, but this is not due solely to a significant rate of divestment. The high propensity for companies to go out of business (legally or otherwise) over the age of 60 is another expression of the fragility of the local economic fabric. In other words, pure and simple cessation without resale is becoming a frequent modality, which certainly limits advancing age, but also constitutes an irreversible failure. The profile of this group is less rural.

In total, these three groups account for 27% of local SMEs and ETIs whose managers are over 65, and present, to varying degrees, very worrying indicators for the renewal of their SME fabric. However, this group is not homogeneous, since it includes rural departments that are in demographic and economic decline, as well as departments within the sphere of influence of major metropolitan areas. With a large workforce and a slightly higher-than-average proportion of older managers, Group D is representative of the national situation in most countries. The absence of a worsening ageing trend can be explained by the often high rates of family transfer. In view of national projections of the age structure by 2026, these must be maintained or even increased to avoid a marked deterioration, or even a drift towards the previous groups. Group E comprises localities, mainly associated with large urban areas. With the exception of a few towns, the proportion of business owners over the age of 65 is well below the national average, and is increasing little.

A demographic equilibrium seems to have been reached, even if the rate of transfers after the age of 60 is relatively low. In areas under the influence of regional metropolises, the creation of SMEs and the transformation of VSEs into SMEs are the main factors stabilizing the age structure from below. The productive fabric is undoubtedly younger in the other departments.

The last two groups are more explicitly part of a virtuous circle of high transferability at the end of professional activity. Group F is associated with medium-density urban areas. In addition to a high frequency of transfers for valuable consideration and family transfers, the use of judicial disappearance or closure by default as a regulatory factor is also higher than average. On the other hand, the option of cessation does not appear to be necessary to avoid the aging of Group G, which is better represented in regional ecosystems traditionally favorable to SMEs. In this case, ensuring optimal renewal of their SME and ETI fabric at the end of their professional activity. The disposal rate for SMEs (excluding VSEs) and SMBs is well above average (2.7%) in real estate (7.8%), information and communication (3.7%), trade, education and health, and business services (3.0%). Conversely, the disposal market is structurally less buoyant in construction (1.7%, with the notable exception of civil engineering), transport and storage (1.9%), personal services (1.9%) and accommodation and catering (2.3%). The industrial divestment rate is in line with the national average, but there are significant disparities within this sector: chemicals, food processing, capital goods, paper, cardboard and metallurgy have higher divestment rates, in contrast to the automotive, plastics and metal products, woodworking and, above all, clothing industries. Although already at an above-average level, divestment rates in the information and communication, real estate, business services and education and health sectors have been on an upward trend over the decade. On the other hand, the proportion of SMEs and SMBs sold in the personal services sector and, to a lesser extent, in the transport and warehousing sector, has been on a downward trend. In the other sectors (industry, construction, trade and accommodation & catering), the rate of divestments has remained broadly constant over the last ten years. The case of farms should also be taken into account. This information is particularly useful in view of the needs already identified locally. For example, isn't it worrying to see a downward trend in transfers in the personal services sector, which is set to expand and is already experiencing recruitment shortages? Furthermore, shouldn't we be keeping a close eye on divestment rates in sectors where advanced countries can make the difference in terms of competitiveness to redress their trade balance, or where questions of economic independence have been raised?

In 2017, the weakening of the local economic fabric in advanced economies was seen more in terms of companies simply disappearing. In the absence of buyers, some companies went out of business, and with them disappeared skills, jobs and know-how. In 2022, a new dimension emerged in the debate: the risk of predation. While the threat of companies disappearing is still very real, there is also the threat of foreign takeovers, with the eventual relocation and loss of technology and know-how to foreign competitors. Of course, it's not a question of demonizing every investor from another country. We need to welcome foreign investment and develop private equity to support local businesses, particularly family businesses, that need to finance their development. However, feedback from the entrepreneurial field points to numerous cases of outright predation, in which companies ultimately disappear from our territories after foreign capital has come to rescue financially fragile businesses.

The risk of predation, linked to the financial fragility of local companies, has obviously increased with the health crisis, during which, as far as predation is concerned, here are a few figures relating to ETIs. In 2021, we recorded a 25% increase in ETI sales compared with 2020; a third of them have been approached. We observe that companies, particularly foreign ones, are approaching local companies because they are interested in their know-how. However, they are not necessarily interested in their site, which they rationalize afterwards. Some takeovers have caused a stir, such as that of the family business Atalian (cleaning services) by the American fund CD&R (Clayton, Dubilier & Rice). Another example is the family firm Demeyère, a furniture manufacturer, bought out by a Moroccan group, Safari. Against a backdrop of crisis, where the question of economic dependence has been raised alongside that of sovereignty, we may well wonder about the ability of territories to protect SMEs and ETIs with a strategic role to play.

It's true that advanced economies have a public economic security policy, based on the interministerial reorganization resulting from decree. These articles state that economic security policy aims to ensure the defense and promotion of economic, industrial and scientific interests, including tangible and intangible assets that are strategic to a country's economy. This includes the defense of digital sovereignty. The Strategic Information and Economic Security Department (SISSE) is responsible for coordinating economic security policy, under the authority of the Commissioner for Strategic Information and Economic Security. Within this framework, SISSE has reinforced its mission of detecting economic security alerts and proposing remedial solutions. In concrete terms, SISSE detected hundreds of economic security alerts in 2021, the overwhelming majority of which (over 2/3) were actually linked to attempts to capture know-how and transfer technology.

When the threat is a proposed takeover by a foreign player, the legal framework of foreign investment control (FIC) is an appropriate response. Regulations have been modernized by law and decree.

Any non-European shareholding in excess of 25% of voting rights - a threshold temporarily lowered to 10% for listed companies during the crisis - (or any takeover for European investors) in companies in sectors deemed strategic is subject to authorization by the Minister for the Economy. On average, a large number of applications were filed under the IEF procedure in 2021, a record year in which the number of applications rose by 31.2% compared with 2020. Investors may be subject to conditions such as maintaining the intellectual property of patents, production and research and development capacities on national soil. This is a major deterrent for investors of uncertain repute.

Economic security thus appears to be well organized, but it seems to target the largest companies, leaving SMEs flying under the radar. Five plans to rebuild economic sovereignty: it is astonishing that the choice was made to limit this lowering of the threshold to local listed companies, effectively excluding SMEs. In fact, all strategic business sectors include a large number of sensitive companies, particularly subcontractors to major groups, which are not listed. This restriction stems from the fact that the capital of listed companies is more widely dispersed than that of unlisted SMEs, exposing the former more than the latter to the risk of an unfriendly transaction (with 10% of the votes, a shareholder could exert significant influence). However, given the impact of the crisis on the financial situation of all companies, and the sovereignty issues involved in a potentially unfriendly foreign takeover of a strategic subcontractor, it is essential to protect unlisted companies in the same way as listed ones. SMEs are essential, not only because they often guarantee independence in terms of subcontracting, but also because they are the future strategic ETIs. Facilitating the transfer of these companies therefore represents both a bulwark against predation, the risk of which is greater in times of crisis, and a weapon for defending the economic sovereignty of countries.

Several measures have been improved to facilitate business transfers. It is important to highlight the importance of the tax system, but also the constraints inherent in certain limitations of the law. In addition, the bills proposed a series of modifications designed in particular to : take account of the increasing number of one-person companies in the economic fabric, remove the condition of unchanged shareholdings in the case of interposed companies between the taxpayer and the company eligible for the transfer scheme, reaffirm the collective commitment deemed acquired (Ecra), the use of which had been progressively limited by the administration, This had given rise to difficulties in terms of legal certainty for many transfer professionals, guaranteeing greater continuity in the event of the death of a shareholder exercising management functions, abolishing annual reporting obligations, providing that a partial breach of the collective or individual undertaking will only result in a pro rata forfeiture, clarifying the possibilities for contributions to a holding company, and better defining the notion of "animating holding company".

The Finance Acts have made the covenant regime more flexible, facilitating inter vivos or inheritance transfers. The changes notably : made it possible to subscribe to a unilateral undertaking to retain shares; relaxed the minimum shareholding threshold for subscribing to a collective undertaking to retain shares; relaxed the conditions under which the collective undertaking to retain shares is deemed to have been acquired without having been formally subscribed, in the presence of an interposed company; made it possible to subscribe to an agreement within six months of the death of the director if the transfer was not anticipated; allowed the beneficiaries of the transfer to contribute their shares to a holding company during the collective undertaking phase, rather than just during the individual undertaking phase; allowed the shares of an interposed company to be contributed to a holding company; considered that a public exchange offer preceding a merger or demerger by less than a year does not affect the individual undertaking to retain; removed the annual obligation to provide the administration with a certificate of compliance with the undertakings, which represented an administrative burden for the beneficiaries of the agreements and proved unnecessary.

In addition to these changes, the covenant regime was the subject of doctrinal clarifications following a public consultation. In response to criticism from practitioners and representative bodies of entrepreneurs, these clarifications were made via the public finance update. The administration has thus withdrawn almost all the grievances raised, but the waiting time (three years between adoption of the Finance Act and publication of the bulletin) was strongly criticized by business leaders, who saw this period of uncertainty as a source of legal uncertainty. The key proposal was to stagger the payment of capital gains tax on the sale of SMEs or ETIs in the event of vendor credit. It was an extension of a measure then reserved for small businesses with sales of less than $2 million and fewer than 10 employees.

A few months later, this measure was included in the Finance Act, authorizing the seller who grants a vendor credit to pay the capital gains tax on the sale at the rate of the scheduled payments made by the buyer, over a maximum period of 5 years. So, depending on whether the vendor loan runs for 2, 3, 4 or 5 years, the tax is now spread over the same period, thereby diluting the financial effort. However, this measure was more limited than the initial proposal, as it applied to small businesses with fewer than 50 employees and total assets or sales not exceeding $10 million. The long-term capital gains concerned are those realized on the sale for valuable consideration of all fixed assets allocated to the exercise of a professional activity or a complete branch of activity, or on the sale of a business, a craft or a customer base. The savings act extended this provision to capital gains realized on the shares of companies that meet the conditions of number of employees and sales or balance sheet.

With regard to the tax credit for employee buy-outs, when employees decide to take over their own company by creating a company dedicated exclusively to the total or partial buy-out, they can benefit from tax assistance in the form of a planned tax credit. For buy-out operations carried out up to December 31, 2022, the conditions have been relaxed, going even further than requested by the companies: the minimum threshold of employees who must hold shares in the new company has been abolished, only a minimum presence requirement has been introduced, and only the voting rights attached to shares in the new company held by one or more persons who, at the date of the buy-out, had been employees of the company bought out for at least eighteen months, are taken into account when calculating the amount of the tax credit.

Lastly, as part of the plan for the self-employed, the Finance Act has eased the tax burden on the transferring entrepreneur, by introducing two exemptions on capital gains: (i) for capital gains arising on the retirement of a business owner or a partner in a company subject to income tax (IR), the period between retirement and sale to benefit from the exemption has been extended from 2 to 3 years from retirement, for business owners claiming their retirement rights in 2019, 2020 and 2021; (ii) for capital gains arising on the transfer of a sole proprietorship or a complete branch of activity, the total and partial capital gains exemption ceilings have been raised to $500,000 and $1,000,000 respectively (compared with $300,000 and $500,000 previously); (iii) finally, it is now possible to transfer or assign the entirety of a business under a management lease to a person other than the tenant manager on retirement or on transfer of the business.

This somewhat mixed picture begs the question as to why there has been such a lack of impetus for business transfers. Since a number of modernization measures have been introduced, what is needed to improve the situation, i.e. to facilitate business transfers? Are further legislative reforms necessary? Are the solutions of a completely different order? What measures should be envisaged to give priority support to managers of selling age in the coming years? Two themes emerge: simplification and security. These two aspects are at the very heart of our missions, and meet the needs expressed by business owners, as well as by the transfer experts who support them in the regions. They underpin a genuine public policy for business transfers. The proposals are based on the principles of simplification and security, and highlight 5 priority objectives, as indicated above: stabilize current legislation to meet the main demand of company directors; safeguard measures that are essential for family transfers and for the development of SMEs and SMIs; simplify procedures and mechanisms to facilitate transfers, particularly employee buyouts; secure transfers by limiting the destabilizing effects of the law, case law or certain administrative decisions; encourage directors to anticipate their transfers.

In such a situation, shouldn't the first priority be to secure transfers? Plans remain essential tools for family transfers. In 2008, among advanced economies, France had an average of 4,500 ETIs, compared with 12,500 in Germany, 10,500 in the UK and 8,000 in Italy. 70% of ETIs are family businesses. It takes an average of 20 years to reach the size of an ETI, a period during which the question of transmission is bound to arise. One out of every two ETIs will pass on in the next few years. In the current situation, difficulties in transferring businesses persist, with 14% of family transfers in France, compared with 50% in Germany and 70% in Italy. Even with the various pacts in place, the gap between France and Italy persists. The insufficient number of ETIs is a handicap for developed countries, insofar as these companies are both rooted in the regions and generally have a strong export presence. In fact, current work on foreign trade has already highlighted the direct link between an improvement in the balance of trade and the development of ETIs, which are an export strike force. As for the territorial logic, it remains, since 70% of ETIs have their head offices in the regions. That's why it's so important to preserve these types of companies, which are the lifeblood of our region. It's worth remembering that 52% of ETIs have a majority family shareholding, and that if we also count minority shareholdings, then 70% of ETIs have a family shareholding.

But the plea for Pacts is not limited to ETIs, as SME managers have no shortage of adjectives to describe them: essential, very important, salutary... Despite the latest measures to modernize the tax system, proposals for changes are still being put forward. In particular, one proposal is for a 90% tax exemption in return for a commitment to retain the shares for 8 or even 10 years. However, the combination of these measures and the 50% reduction in duties on gifts made before the age of 70 in certain countries can already result in an exemption from free transfer duties of around 90% of the value of the company transferred, or even more, depending on its value. So, by opting for a higher exemption rate, the legislator would be tending to favor a virtually zero-rate transfer. In addition to the delicate question of the constitutionality of such a measure, which has never been settled, it is appropriate to question the relevance of such a proposal in a context of attacks often abusively assimilating private and professional assets, and considering the company as a privilege. To go any further in the exemption would run the risk of achieving a result contrary to the desired effect: the durability of these pacts would be called into question, whereas it is precisely they that are to be protected. This chapter has opted for sanctuarization, in the knowledge that it is more necessary than ever to reaffirm the vital need to preserve these mechanisms to support the transfer of business and know-how in advanced economies.

On the other hand, it should be noted that too little is known about the mechanism, not only among managers - especially of SMEs - but also among some experts in the field of business transfers. For the former, the mechanism is simply too often unknown; for the latter, the reforms introduced by the Finance Act have not necessarily yet been assimilated. A very recent survey by ExpertActions Group highlights this lack of knowledge in an alarming way: 82% of managers questioned are not at all familiar with the system! It therefore seems urgent, both to establish the legitimacy of these mechanisms and to simplify their approach, to organize a nationwide information campaign aimed at company directors, involving all support experts. To help achieve this, we will be working on an information film to be posted on our website. Making the scheme known to as many business owners as possible will not only help to facilitate transfers, but also make this tax scheme more secure. Naturally, such a campaign will also be used to present other schemes that encourage transfers, whether within the family or to a third party, employee or otherwise. The Chartered accountants will play a key role in informing and popularizing the possibilities offered by the General Tax Code. It would be useful, for example, for chartered accountants to highlight the latest reforms that have modernized these tools; the possibility offered to a manager who has sold his company to his children to continue working for the company; the possibility of combining the scheme with the $100,000 allowance per parent and per child for direct line transfers; and payment facilities such as the 5-year suspension and ten-year spreading of payments.

In addition, we need to draw attention to the need to clarify the notion of a group holding company, for which the law offers only a vague definition that is insufficiently operational for its implementation within the framework of the scheme. For several years now, this point has been identified by company directors as a source of legal uncertainty, which does not only concern large groups - quite the contrary. In 2017, over 33% of SMEs with between 10 and 100 employees, and 62% of SMEs with between 100 and 250 employees, were held by a holding company. Furthermore, an analysis of corporate groups reveals that, on average, they are predominantly small in several countries: out of a total of almost 134,000 groups, there are just 289 large groups, 5,600 intermediate-sized groups, 65,700 small or medium-sized groups and 62,400 microgroups (i.e. with fewer than 10 employees and annual sales or balance sheet total not exceeding $2 million). Given the number of SMEs concerned, and the tax arrangements applicable to holding companies recognized as animating subsidiaries, the notion of an animating holding company appears crucial.

This is precisely the case when it comes to eligibility for the scheme. For some players, legal clarification is not necessary, given that the notion of "animation" and its consequences have been defined by case law and administrative doctrine. While there is no denying the efforts made by tax authorities and judges to clarify the concept, the definition of group leadership and the way it is taken into account in the application of certain tax provisions remain unstable. It should be remembered that an initial definition appeared in the General Tax Code relating to the solidarity tax on wealth (ISF), which has since been repealed. This definition was taken up again in the Finance Act, which however removed the term "holding animatrice" (animating holding company) from the article relating to the real estate wealth tax (IFI) (real estate wealth tax). These are companies which, in addition to managing a portfolio of holdings, have as their principal activity: active participation in the management of their group's policy and in the control of their subsidiaries carrying on a commercial, industrial, craft, agricultural or professional activity; where applicable, the provision of specific administrative, legal, accounting, financial and real estate services to these subsidiaries.

Despite this legal basis, the clarifications made to the concept of a "holding animatrice" and its application have been the subject of constant movement between the doctrine of the tax authorities and that of various judges, highlighting, until very recently, the considerable legal uncertainty inherent in this situation. The most recent clashes illustrating this legal instability are: the decision by the higher courts to reject the quantitative criteria hitherto used by the tax authorities. In fact, the latter considered that the "animation" nature of the business was assessed on the basis of two cumulative criteria: the sales generated by this activity (at least 50% of total sales) and the amount of gross fixed assets (at least 50% of total gross assets). Judges have rejected this administrative interpretation, preferring a set of indicators based on the nature of the business and the conditions under which it is carried out, rather than on simple accounting ratios. In its ruling, the Commercial Chamber held that the holding company's loss of its role as group coordinator before the expiry of the legal period for retaining shares (individual undertaking), could not in law render the transfer of the holding company's shares ineligible for the scheme.

It thus overturned the court's decision, ruling that the latter had added a condition to the law that it did not contain, and thus violated the provisions of the article. This ruling curtly censures the previous decision, which had supported the tax authorities in their decision to call into question an exemption granted to a company, on the grounds that, after having resold shares representing 83% of the group's total sales, its holding company was engaged in a purely financial activity. This ruling should be seen as a firm reminder to the tax authorities, which have made a habit of using questionable analyses to add requirements not provided for in the legislation.

The message is clear: tax authorities must adhere to legal requirements. This decision by the court profoundly calls into question the logic of the scheme, and in particular its objective of ensuring the long-term viability of the company. In addition, it could create a windfall effect by allowing gift-divestiture transactions to purge unrealized capital gains, while leaving the beneficiaries of the transfer free to dispose of the cash generated by the proceeds from the company's shares.

For these reasons, the article was amended to make the actual maintenance of the group's animation activity during the legal holding period a condition for benefiting from the preferential regime. This amendment, regarded as an anti-abuse measure, was maintained. These two examples of reversals show that tax authorities and judges can have very different interpretations of the conditions for implementing these mechanisms, and in particular of the notion of "animating holding company". The last case is particularly striking, since the French Supreme Court censured the administration's interpretation of the law, forcing the legislator to amend the text of the article, thereby giving a legal basis to the administrative doctrine.

These developments underline the instability and legal uncertainty surrounding the notion of "animating holding company", which can have serious economic consequences for those involved in business transfers, particularly in terms of the collection of transfer duties. ExpertActions had recommended that the definition of the concept of "animating holding company" be clarified in law, by specifying the conditions for presumption of animation and control of a subsidiary. The aim of this recommendation was not only to stabilize the concept in law, but also to make it legally more secure, in order to limit the financial difficulties that would result for companies. In the light of recent case law, the need for legal certainty is more crucial than ever for business transfers. Indeed, an amendment tabled shows that new questions could arise in the event of a new dispute: the amendment, which was rejected, proposed that the loss of the status of "animation" should not necessarily lead to the loss of the exemption, but only to a pro rata loss of holdings held by the holding company in companies with an operational activity. This position could be examined differently by the judge without further legislative precision.

The instability suffered by managers is not solely due to a lack of legislative definition. Numerous testimonials have highlighted the difficulties associated with the tax authorities' assessment of their company. In addition to the question of the company's valuation, it is the tax authorities' assessment of the animating nature of holding companies that raises difficulties. The disarray felt by the directors interviewed stems either from an excessively long wait for a response from the authorities, sometimes delaying the planned transfer schedule, or from a reversal of a previously established position. The reassessments they sometimes have to face are obviously destabilizing, both for themselves and for their company, when in good faith they thought that the constituent elements of their transfer project had been definitively validated. It is therefore proposed to introduce a specific rescript procedure for the recognition of a holding company's status, with a maximum time limit of 6 months. This system would enable managers who so wish to give greater security to their disposal plans. To complement this system, and to reduce the risk associated with personal assessments that sometimes differ within the same department, it is also recommended that a "transfer" referent be appointed within each regional public finance department. In addition to providing security, the specific rescript procedure aims to establish a constructive economic dialogue between the administration and company directors.

The abolition of the system of prior information for employees therefore represents a real risk of destabilization. The system of compulsory prior information remains in place, even though the strongest advocates of employee buy-outs themselves recognize that it is unsuitable because it is disconnected from the realities of company life, and even dangerous for buy-out projects insofar as the information creates a wind of panic that is detrimental to the health of the company, which is thus destabilized. This system, which was designed to support employees, has unfortunately failed to achieve its objective, as the essential element in the transfer of a company to one or more employees is trust, not forced information. It is therefore proposed to repeal the provisions of the Commercial Code resulting from the articles of the law (the provisions of these two articles governing employee information respectively in companies required to set up a works council and in those not subject to this obligation). Because support for employee buyouts is essential to a genuine public policy on business transfers, it must be backed up by incentives to encourage more employees to embark on the adventure of taking over a company. This is the purpose of the measures presented in the next chapter.

We also need to secure financing mechanisms for business transfers. Financing agencies play an essential role in public policy on business transfers. With their guarantee schemes, these structures cover takeover projects for VSEs, SMEs and businesses. Two types of guarantee are available to help buyers: as the name suggests, the start-up guarantee covers takeover projects involving the purchase of business assets or shares, and is aimed at SMEs less than 3 years old. These takeovers account for 27% of operations covered by this type of guarantee, compared with 73% for ex-nihilo creations; the transmission guarantee is aimed either at helping new entrepreneurs to set up in business, through the purchase of an SME or a business, by facilitating their access to bank credit, or at facilitating the development of existing companies through external growth. On average, 5,200 companies benefit from these schemes every year in developed countries (90% of which are very small businesses).

A scientific study on the impact of institutional guarantees on business transfers has demonstrated their positive effects. Overall, the financing structure guarantees banks up to 40% to 70%, with the support of regional funds, to finance VSEs and SMEs in the riskiest phases (takeover and transfer, innovation, international, etc.). In addition, the Prêt-transmission is an invaluable tool, recognized by players in the field, to facilitate the takeover of VSEs and SMEs. Working in partnership with regional authorities, the financing agency offers a loan to finance the takeover or transfer of a business, with no guarantee on the company's assets or the manager's wealth. This loan finances projects worth between $40,000 and $1,500,000 over a period of 5 to 7 years, with a guaranteed loan-to-value ratio of up to 80%. It is therefore the financing agency's tool, combined with assistance from the regions, which comes closest to what some might call business recovery support. However, some regions have decided not to set up a Prêt-transmission. As a result, this loan is not available throughout the country. What's more, the characteristics of the loan are not identical in all the regions that have decided to introduce it. For the sake of harmonization, it would be useful to roll out an identical offer throughout France for VSEs and SMEs.

The financing of institutional guarantees and unsecured loans was historically budgeted under the Business Development and Regulation program. Until the next Finance Bill, these credits were carried by a Business Financing action. After a period of decline, the line devoted to the budgetary financing of the institutional guarantee was systematically deleted in the Finance Bill - and then reinstated - albeit in much smaller amounts than before (down to the symbolic sum of $10,000). It is worth recalling the context of this debudgetization, with the ordinance reorganizing the public investment structure and amending the ordinance relating to the public investment structure, which authorized the absorption of the structure by its subsidiary. At the same time as this reorganization, certain decision-makers wanted the guarantee business to be financed by its dividends.

If financing is guaranteed until the end of the year through the economic stimulus package in certain countries, the question of funding will once again arise. In fact, for the time being, an average of $464 million in credit has been allocated, to which have been added the redeployment of guarantee fund balances, redeployments linked to the merger of structures and the recycling of dividends not paid to the State. From an operational point of view, the decision to abolish the budget line poses a real financing challenge. The existence of a budget line within the general budget makes it possible to support an activity that is essential to the health of the economy. In the event of the budget line's definitive disappearance, the uncertainty of a financing system based exclusively on dividends would lead the company to revise downwards the risk taken in each guarantee granted - it could go as low as 30%. Given the crucial role of guarantees, this prospect would be a cataclysm for business transfers.

Over and above the economic issue, there is also the question of parliamentary oversight of public-sector structures. For several years now, guarantee fund financing methods have been the subject of budgetary subterfuge. It is imperative that parliamentarians be better informed on this subject. The public funds earmarked for these guarantees represent very large sums. In some countries, the scope of the documents appended to the finance bill needs to be extended. Guarantee activities are in fact financed by public funds, which means that parliamentary authorization and control cannot always be fully exercised. At a time when it is desirable to assert the need for a genuine public policy on business transfers, it seems strange, to say the least, to remove the budget line that not only guarantees but also measures the public guarantee effort for VSEs and SMEs, which is essential for business takeovers. It is therefore proposed to secure the guarantee activity of public financing structures, so useful in its "transfer" aspect, and to finance the national deployment of the "Transfer Loan" by reinstating the action of the Business Development program of the Economy Mission within the next Finance Act, and to vote sufficient credits to perpetuate these mechanisms (bank guarantee and Transfer Loan) for the benefit of VSEs and SMEs.

We should also seek to make the deductibility of goodwill amortization permanent. The article in the French Finance Act enshrines a general principle of non-deductibility of goodwill amortization for tax purposes, while providing a temporary exception to this principle. Accordingly, depreciation recorded in company accounts for goodwill acquired between January 1, 2022 and December 31, 2025 will be deductible. Lastly, the same article provides for a government report to assess the cost of this measure, before July 1, 2025. The parliamentary debates highlighted the link between this derogation and the economic recovery phase following the health crisis. The considerations that prevailed in adopting this derogation could also have taken into account the strong risk that the non-transmission of companies, particularly businesses, poses for the vitality of local areas. This risk is highlighted by an ExpertActions Group study on the impact of bank guarantees on business transfers. It points out that nearly 30% of managers who succeeded in taking over a business encountered serious financial difficulties in their takeover project. It therefore seems necessary to make this measure permanent in order to take account of the challenges of business transfers in the regions.

With regard to the harmonization of registration fees, we would point out that the existence of different rates, depending on the form of company (sale of shares: 3%; or sale of shares: 0.1%), can lead to changes in the articles of association with a view to tax optimization, sometimes resulting in underestimated costs (such as the cost of compulsory auditing). This is a perverse and counter-productive effect. Moreover, the rate also varies for goodwill (from 0% to 5%), depending on the level of the acquisition price. It is proposed to simplify the transfer by harmonizing these rates and setting all registration fees at 0.1%.

Measures aimed at facilitating and simplifying employee buy-outs should provide a concrete and effective incentive, echoing the repeal of the obligation to provide prior information. Three components can be mentioned here: tax credit, tax allowance, and employee takeover training. The relaxation of the conditions governing the tax credit for employee buyouts was inspired by recent developments. Indeed, the Finance Act abolished the requirement for buyouts to be carried out by 15 employees, or 30% of employees where the workforce does not exceed 50, and replaced it with a more general requirement for buyouts to be carried out by one or more people who, at the date of the buyout, had been employees of the acquired company for at least eighteen months. While this is a welcome step forward, it should be noted that, on average, only 45 companies benefited from this tax credit in 2006, for an average annual expenditure of less than $500,000. The

Finance Act also extended the scheme. It is proposed that this scheme be made permanent, so as not to discourage employee takeovers.

Given the extremely low level of take-up of this scheme, it can be deduced that the article's relaxation was not sufficient. It is therefore proposed to increase the tax allowances (from $300,000 to $500,000) for the acquisition by one or more employees of a craft business, a business, an agricultural business or the customer base of a sole proprietorship, or of shares in a company: on the basis of the article, in the case of a gift in full ownership; on the basis of the article, in the case of a transfer in full ownership. Finally, let's highlight the need to train employees wishing to embark on the adventure of taking over a company, which is unfortunately more complex to grasp than setting up a new business from an administrative point of view, but often much more rewarding from an economic point of view for the region. As such training can be costly, it is proposed to encourage the allocation of additional rights to the personal training account by the various players identified in the article of the Labour Code (State, skills operators, regions, local authorities, employers, etc.).

These measures should do more to encourage employee buyouts, which are often a successful gamble. Even today, employee buy-outs can appear to be the ideal solution for preserving jobs, know-how and corporate culture beyond the family circle. This is the case, for example, of Rairies Montrieux, a manufacturer of terracotta building materials with the Living Heritage label. After having been a family business for 5 generations, it is finally being passed on to 5 managers during a transition period currently underway, led by the current CEO, the last family manager. A fast-growing specialist in bio-solutions for the agricultural sector, the company has been developing since 1989 on the foundations of an ESOP (Employee Stock Purchase), which enables it to drive its own strategy by controlling its own capital. This strategy has enabled the company to develop a powerful R&D and CSR (Corporate Social Responsibility) policy. This company is an exemplary example of how employee buyouts and the promotion of employee share ownership can be win-win formulas. Managers should also be encouraged to think ahead. The "advice cheque for transmission " scheme is directly inspired by the " cheque to support sale or takeover " scheme, which can cover costs relating to: valuing the business; finding counterparties; drawing up a transfer agreement; legal advice; and carrying out financial, social or environmental audits. Eligible costs also include strategic support and management advice for the buyer during a post-takeover period of up to three years from the date of signature of the transfer agreement. In Wallonia, the total amount of public assistance granted per beneficiary over three years as part of the business transfer voucher scheme is limited to $22,000. This measure seems much more effective than the one that simply proposed a deduction for diagnostic costs, since receiving a message telling the manager that he or she can benefit from such a voucher from the age of 55 onwards should help raise awareness of the issues at stake and encourage better anticipation. If the offer is made up to the manager's 65th birthday, it is to be hoped that he or she will not wait until the last moment to organize the transfer of his or her business.

We must not forget to facilitate the transfer to a sustainability fund. Created by law, the sustainability fund is made up of the free and irrevocable contribution of capital securities or shares in one or more companies carrying on an industrial, commercial, craft or agricultural activity, or holding direct or indirect equity interests in one or more companies carrying on such an activity, set up by one or more founders so that the fund manages these shares, exercises the rights attached to them and uses its resources to contribute to the economic survival of the company or companies in question, and to carry out or finance works or missions in the public interest. This fund seems to suffer from an overly restrictive legal and tax framework. The free transfer of shares to a sustainability fund is subject to transfer duty at a rate of 60%, and capital gains realized by legal entities are taxable under ordinary law (but may be deferred under certain conditions). Contributions of company shares to the sustainability fund should therefore be exempt from transfer duties.

Alternatively, introduce a tax deferral system for gratuitous transfer duties, and clarify the conditions for the applicability of institutional mechanisms to legal entities making contributions.

It is also regrettable that the wording of the law leaves room for doubt as to whether the founder of a sustainability fund is an individual or a legal entity, which should also be clarified given the number of companies held by a holding company (i.e. a legal entity). The tax deferral regime for the transfer of shares by legal entities to a sustainability fund should be amended rapidly, so that it applies to all contributions (and not just those made when the fund was set up).

It is also essential to organize the coordination of local transmission players. Numerous initiatives exist in all regions, but there is sometimes an impression of overlapping actions and a lack of effective coordination. The organization of meetings, whether physical or virtual, is to be commended. In addition, each player is developing its own database of potential buyers or businesses to be transferred. What's more, each major player offers a wealth of information on its own website, without this information being fully coordinated or at least linked to one another. Managers, and especially buyers, feel lost when faced with an avalanche of information, data sources and contacts. Given the multitude of players involved for any manager wishing to sell or take over a business, it is tempting to propose a one-stop shop. However, a coordination strategy would be more appropriate, and would be based on several elements. Firstly, it would be desirable to define a national charter between all public and private players (chartered accountants, regions, banks, etc.) detailing the principles for relaying information between them (in particular, the rules for securing confidential data on companies to be sold) and for coordinating measures and aid, as well as the application of these principles at regional level.

Since the objectives of the business transfer process can be aligned with national priorities, it is conceivable that the charter could include a formal commitment to business transfer, and a strategy to promote business takeovers, with a particular focus on: preserving know-how, developing forward-looking sectors, defending strategic interests for countries (defending economic sovereignty, foreign trade recovery objectives), and lastly, it could include training and awareness-raising objectives to encourage female entrepreneurship (only 7% of business takeovers are currently carried out by women). The charter could then define how these principles and actions are to be applied at local level. The administrations concerned would undertake to develop a real policy of advice and support for managers, going well beyond the logic of control or even sanction.

This regional approach could be based on the appointment of referents in each region, who would be the preferred contacts for managers selling and acquiring businesses: a referent responsible for collecting information on businesses to be sold or acquired from private players (e.g., chambers of commerce and industry), and a referent for public players (e.g., the region's director of economic services). The public referent in particular should facilitate dialogue with all the relevant administrations (tax aspects for valuation, eligibility for aid and guarantees, deadlines for compliance with standards, etc.). Finally, the information transmitted between players should be used to better account for transmissions, to compensate for the current lack of statistics. National consolidation could be entrusted to an existing structure.

Chapter 4

Foreign trade and social entrepreneurship: the urgent need for a public strategy

> With the trade deficit widening again in most developed countries, it is important to understand the causes of this phenomenon, and to suggest ways of remedying the difficulties faced by SMEs (small and medium-sized enterprises) and ETIs (intermediate-sized enterprises) in terms of foreign trade. The year 2021 was marked by an average trade deficit of several billion dollars, further deteriorating the position of certain countries. Figures for the first quarters of the year show a new record deficit.

This situation is alarming because: the deterioration is not sudden (it is the result of a long process induced by the political choice to deindustrialize certain countries over the last 40 years, and has simply worsened with the recent health and energy crises); dependence on imports is not only costly, but also calls into question the sovereignty of States; decisions to relocate cannot be taken without taking into account numerous factors of competitiveness - notably non-cost factors (skills, innovation, etc.) - which are currently too neglected. Many risks are underestimated for companies and for economic performance, such as vulnerabilities in terms of supply, the relocation of services and tele-migration, the potential impact of European decisions on standards, etc. 10 measures, both strategic and operational, have been formulated to remedy this situation in the long term, and ensure that these countries no longer suffer their continued downgrading in terms of foreign trade. To be proactive, these countries need to be more forward-looking and visionary.

For the past twenty years, these countries have watched helplessly as the goods trade deficit has widened. It was around two decades ago that the balance of trade in goods was last in surplus, and the widening has already accelerated in several phases. Although recent figures have been exacerbated by the health and energy crises (-$26.7 billion on average between 2019 and 2021, then -$65.3 billion on average in the first three quarters of this year, with a very heavy deficit in the energy sector), the continuing deterioration is a direct result of the de-industrialization of advanced economies, a strategic choice made by many governments over the last 40 years and highlighted by all economists.

For example, industry's share of GDP fell by 10 points in France to 13.5% in 2019, compared with 24.2% in Germany, 19.6% in Italy and 15.8% in Spain. In Germany, the number of industrial jobs is 7 million, more than double the number in France (3.2 million). They highlight the trade balances of EU member states, ranking them by deficit on the left and surplus on the right. France is last in the Union in 2021 (-$84.7 billion or -$109 billion according to the dollarstat calculation method), while Germany has the biggest surplus ($173.3 billion or $178.4 billion according to dollarstat). However, a pronounced slowdown has recently been observed in Germany, with the first monthly trade deficit since reunification (1991) in May 2022.

Alongside the deficit in the balance of goods, there will be a surplus in the balance of services of $36.2 billion in 2021, driven by transportation and business services. Between 2001 and 2021, service exports increased by 140%, or twice as much as goods exports, rising from 24% to 33% of total exports. What's more, services and goods are intrinsically linked, since 40% of the value added incorporated in goods exports is made up of services. However, the surplus on the services balance is unable, overall, to offset the deficit on the trade balance, as shown by the evolution of the current account balance. Although 2021 saw a surplus of $9 billion, the first quarters of 2022 saw a succession of deficits (a deficit of $18.3 billion in the third quarter of 2022). To fully understand the issues involved in foreign trade, we need to define the various components referred to.

Finally, France's international investment position continues to deteriorate, rising from -$709.4 billion in 2020 to -$801.9 billion in 2021. The Bank points out that this represents 32.3% of GDP, bringing it close to the alert threshold defined by the European macroeconomic imbalance procedure (deficit of 35% of GDP). In view of these facts, any action aimed at improving developed countries' foreign trade must be preceded by strategic reflection on the following questions: What are the concrete objectives in terms of sovereignty? What should be the priorities in terms of independence? Relocation or development of production: what are the advantages in terms of competitiveness, which sectors should be favored and what skills are needed to achieve them? Do they have all the tools they need to analyze regional and foreign market opportunities? How can we identify companies likely to succeed in the internationalization challenge and make a useful contribution to export development?

There is a lack of strategic vision when it comes to foreign trade issues. The risk of relocation of services, particularly with the development of digital technologies. Today, efforts in training and skills development are not sufficient to avoid the threat of telemigration. As services are linked to exported goods, their fate depends on reindustrialization, and therefore on the long-term development of local SMEs and ETIs. This reindustrialization will only be sustainable if companies are profitable, despite the current constraints of standards, employment costs and tax pressures. It must also take into account companies that promote their country's sovereignty.

The risk of dependency is underestimated. Firstly, in terms of intellectual property, since we depend on data centers located abroad. Secondly, supply vulnerabilities are downplayed. Indeed, local studies (Treasury, etc) only take into account data available to customs; thus, the risk is considered insignificant when a product is imported from a regional country, even though its components come from countries identified as more risky. Non-price competitiveness is poorly understood, whereas the focus should be on all factors in this dimension: normative environment, characteristics of importing companies, range positioning, qualifications, and innovation.

All too often, local companies are not even supported. Public purchasers give priority almost exclusively to the lowest bidder in public procurement contracts, whereas they could take into account other criteria on which local companies perform well (the health crisis has highlighted this inconsistency). What's more, large local companies don't have the culture of "hunting in packs" - which consists in conquering foreign markets by dragging along ETIs or SMEs of the same nationality - that is so effective in Germany and Italy.

Finally, public administration does not support companies; on the contrary, it is too often punitive, unlike its German and Italian counterparts. The impact of decisions, particularly in terms of standards, seems to be overlooked. And yet, without a commercial strategy that promotes reciprocity of obligations, they are likely to further reduce the competitiveness of companies. Overtransposition must be eliminated, and mirror clauses between locally manufactured and imported products must be enforced.

There is no shortage of formulas used by economists to describe the phenomena induced by deindustrialization: a "vicious circle" (endemic unemployment, weakened innovation, etc.) or an "infernal triptych" (weak workforce skills, higher wage costs, tax pressure on companies).

Yet supporting companies in their export drive seems to be disconnected from these considerations, which call for a cross-functional analysis and a strategy that cuts across all public policies that have an impact on company competitiveness. This is what emerges from analyses of the role of strategic export institutions, whose strategic dimension seems paradoxically to have been overlooked. The steering of public policies, which one might expect from this body, is non-existent, leaving only a monitoring body (as was the case for the export measures of the stimulus plan).

The government's foreign trade strategy is aimed at transforming the export support model for VSEs, SMEs and ETIs. The public policy of supporting companies is presented as one of three levels of action, alongside policies in favor of competitiveness and the articulation of export priorities at sector level. This reform has given rise to Team Export, which brings together all the public solutions offered by the regions, government departments and Chambers of Commerce and Industry to support local companies in their international expansion. With 250 regional advisors and 750 international advisors, this network aims to offer effective assistance to local companies, notably via a one-stop shop. Financial support comes in a variety of forms: direct government financing (Treasury loans, private sector study and assistance funds), export credits (export credit, international unsecured loans), public guarantees for foreign trade (export credit insurance, prospecting insurance), international volunteer work for companies.

Despite these advances, which are appreciated in the field, it must be emphasized that the players and their support offerings are still too little known and insufficiently coordinated. What's more, there seems to be no solid strategy for choosing which companies to support, and an obsession with numbers to the detriment of long-term effectiveness. In these countries, there will be an average of 135,900 local exporting companies in 2021, and 139,400 in the first quarter of 2022. On average, just 1,000 companies would account for 70% of exported added value. ETIs appear to be the strike force alongside large companies. However, the objective of increasing the number of exporting companies, particularly first- time exporters, seems to prevail, even though their contribution to export growth is not always decisive. What's more, there are too few mid-sized companies in these advanced economies (5,400 in France, 12,500 in Germany and 8,000 in Italy), and the framework for business transfers is not sufficiently attractive for SMEs to grow. Yet they should be a priority for the development of international trade. Finally, a comparison with Germany and Italy shows that these countries offer more free support measures, such as the participation of national companies in international trade fairs.

Hence the need to define renewed strategic approaches: define, via an economic orientation law, a long- term strategy (2040 as a minimum) to establish foreign trade objectives - and economic sovereignty - and identify the sectors, skills and companies to support; renovate the governance of strategic export councils to enable them to effectively steer national strategies, by integrating foreign trade objectives into the various public policies that have an impact on the balance of trade, and ensuring effective coordination between these policies; strengthen coordination between members of Team Export -- TE -- and present the results of their actions to the renovated strategic export council; better integrate the issue of services into the fight against relocation.

Also, in operational terms : facilitate business transfers and support SMEs and SMIs to encourage relocation and local re-industrialization; encourage companies to hunt in packs; organize an information campaign on the support services offered to SMEs and SMIs by members of Team Export and make participation in international trade fairs free of charge for local companies; reinforce language learning and knowledge of economics, mathematics, technology and international trade in secondary and higher education; better identify the risks of supply vulnerabilities using regional customs data; define the content, framework and ethical rules for the creation and operation of a database which, together with artificial intelligence, will make it possible to finely assist local SMEs in exporting; entrust the management of this database to one of the TE players, in compliance with economic intelligence rules.

To better understand this issue, it is also important to look back at the continuing deterioration in the balance of trade in goods. Foreign trade and the internationalization of SMEs and ETIs is a dimension that often evokes the factors weighing on the competitiveness of local companies in a context of heightened competition. Estimates for the year show a record trade deficit averaging $84.7 billion. This compares with an average of $64.7

billion last year and $58 billion the year before, an average widening of nearly $26.7 billion in two years.

In an economic context marked by successive exceptional crises (health, energy), one might have thought that this accelerated deterioration in the balance of trade was purely cyclical. Sectoral balances, moreover, highlight the weight of the deficit in the energy sector. However, this accelerated deterioration is not the first. Between 2002 and 2020, imports grew by an average of $171.1 billion, twice as fast as exports over the same period (+$94.8 billion on average). The trade deficit widened most between 2003 and 2011. Then, after a relative improvement, it widened again from 2016 onwards.

For the past 20 years, advanced economies have watched helplessly as their trade balances widened. And the economic crisis of 2022 will further cripple them, as estimates predict an average deficit of over $150 billion. There is one nuance, however: the balance of foreign trade in services (the other component of the current account balance) is positive. It will even be significantly higher in 2021, with an average of $36.2 billion, compared with an average of $19 billion in 2020 and $30.4 billion in 2019. This figure is mainly driven by transportation services, but also by business services (technical, professional and management consulting services). However, this surplus on the services balance is not enough to offset the deficit on the goods balance. Thus, it is the balance of trade in goods that weighs on the foreign trade balance of advanced countries. It will be in deficit by an average of $48.6 billion in 2021. Given the economic crisis affecting certain regions, it might be tempting to reassure ourselves by comparing ourselves with other partners. Unfortunately, observation of the global situation only reinforces the feeling that we're at an impasse when it comes to foreign trade. As can be seen from the representation of the trade balances of these member countries, the comparison reveals the seriousness of the situation. The lowest-ranked in 2021 average - 109 billion, while the highest-ranked have the biggest surpluses (178.4 billion on average). However, a pronounced slowdown has recently been observed among the best-in-class, with the first monthly trade deficits in May 2022. The deterioration in the trade balance has been much more marked in some countries than in others, and therefore in relation to their main trading partners. Between 2002 and 2020, the trade balance widened by an average of $89.9 billion, while over the same period, the surplus of leading partners increased by an average of $55 billion.

Dependence on imports from China is blatantly obvious in France, Germany, Italy, Belgium, Spain and the Netherlands. These countries will account for 72% of advanced economies' exports in 2021. There is therefore a regional concentration of exports from certain countries. However, their markets are growing more slowly than the rest of the world, particularly Asia. For ExpertActios Group, the deterioration in the regional performance of countries should be seen in the context of the erosion of their market share in global goods exports, from 4.9% in 2000 to 3.5% in 2020, in 2021. These losses are greater than those recorded globally in advanced countries. The latter accounted for 69.2% of export market share in 2000 and 54.9% in 2015.

The deterioration in local foreign trade cannot be understood without mentioning the rise of emerging economies. The rise of these economies in world trade has affected all advanced countries, but some countries in particular have lost more market share than their main partners. The decline in market share linked to the development of emerging economies was assessed on the basis of modelling carried out by ExpertActions Group in 2016, the findings of which can be summarized as follows: between 2000 and 2015, some of these countries experienced a 29% decline in their export market share on the extra- regional manufactured goods market, which can be explained almost entirely by the rise of emerging economies; competition from emerging countries also explains half of the decline in regional market share in manufactured goods exports (a decline of 21% between 2000 and 2015).

China's entry into global competition has thus altered the distribution of world market shares. China became a member of the WTO on December 11, 2001. Barriers to trade, in the form of quantitative restrictions or customs duties, were largely lifted in accordance with the accession agreement. As a result, tariffs on imports from China have fallen from an average of 16.4% in 2000 - the year before China joined the WTO - to 5.4% in 2019. Since China's accession to the WTO, some of our trade deficits with that country have grown significantly. It has increased almost fivefold (an average of +$21.4 billion between 2000 and 2019). Most of this increase in the bilateral trade deficit occurred in the decade following China's accession to the WTO. In 2009, China became the world's leading exporter, ahead of Germany. Emerging economies have accelerated their move upmarket, and competition is all the more fierce as trade practices (including counterfeiting) and social, health and environmental standards are less demanding.

We must also stress the structural problem of competitiveness. Indeed, most of these countries' export underperformance is attributable to insufficient price (or cost) and non-price (non-cost) competitiveness. Competitiveness, which is now a handicap against the backdrop of the rise of China and emerging countries, had already been the source of the gap with Germany. The cost competitiveness of the most exposed countries was the main handicap, with unit labor costs (ULC) growing at three times the rate of the best-performing countries. The margin rate of manufacturing companies in several countries fell by 2.4 points of value added over the period 2000-2007, while that of the best-performing companies rose by 8.2 points over the same period. In addition, the wage moderation and pension reduction policies of the leading countries in the 2000s not only enabled them to gain in cost-competitiveness in a context of fixed exchange rates, but also to limit the dynamics of income and hence domestic demand. Between 2000 and 2008, domestic demand in the worst-performing countries rose by 16.6%, compared with 3.5% for the leaders.

One of the main themes of this article was the way in which follower countries have fallen behind leader countries: this is due to the reduction in working hours in some countries, to a general system of corporate taxation, and then to cost competitiveness, which has put several countries on different trajectories. But we then saw a convergence in labor costs, with the high-performing countries catching up - with the introduction of a minimum wage in particular - combined with policies to lower labor costs in the low-performing countries. For example, the CICE tax credit (tax credit for competitiveness and employment) deducted part of the wage bill from the tax burden, before being transformed into a permanent reduction in employer contributions.

Non-cost competitiveness, on the other hand, remains a handicap. Despite the convergence of unit labor costs, imbalances are not being reduced, which means that the problem in some of these countries is a lack of non-cost competitiveness - in a way, the sum of our ignorance. Non-cost competitiveness is everything that can't be explained by costs, i.e., many things - quality, governance, etc. - that are difficult to quantify and on which our ignorance is based. --which are difficult to quantify, and on which it is also difficult to act. These countries therefore very probably have a problem of non-price competitiveness, meaning that they need to continue their efforts in R&D and education. The leaders have a very high level of technological R&D investment. There's no secret about it: if you want non-price competitiveness, you need quality, even if, in the end, the two types of competitiveness always converge, because with equal quality, it's always price that makes the difference.

The analysis also highlights a shortcoming in public policy: insufficient identification of risks, both past and present. Whether we're talking about the de-industrialization of recent decades, supply difficulties or sovereignty issues, the feeling is one of a lack of political analysis and anticipation of risks to the economy. The recent trade balance figures have certainly been aggravated by the health and energy crises (-$26.7 billion on average between 2019 and 2021, then -$65.3 billion on average in the first three quarters of 2022, with a very heavy deficit in the energy sector), but the phenomenon of continuous deterioration is the direct result of deindustrialization, a strategic choice assumed by many governments over the past 40 years and pointed out by all economists. Indeed, among the causes of the deficit, the one that immediately comes to mind is that of deindustrialization: strategic error, drift, abandonment of industrial strategy, deindustrialization to be deplored, and so on. For example, industry's share of GDP has fallen by 10 points to 13.5% in 2019 in France, 24.2% in Germany, 19.6% in Italy and 15.8% in Spain. In Germany, the number of industrial jobs is 7 million, more than double the average for other countries. While there is unanimous agreement that certain countries have made strategic choices in the past, it is not so easy to identify the consequences and solutions.

Deindustrialization has disastrous consequences: the multiplication of zones of endemic unemployment, a vicious circle not only in terms of the innovation process but also of skills development, in short, an impoverishment of the economy and a greatly reduced ability to bounce back from shocks such as the health crisis. These issues of de-industrialization and external deficit have long remained blind spots in economists' work, and this applies equally to work on international macroeconomics and international trade. So-called Ricardian models of international trade are not interested in the question of external deficits, because these models are by nature balanced, i.e. exports equal imports, and so trade deficits are not an object of study, which is rather paradoxical when you look at traditional macroeconomic models, i.e. neo-classical models, which consider deficits as an advantage because they allow you to consume more than you produce. The problem with this type of model is that it neglects the dynamic effects of deficits on production structures, in this case on deindustrialization.

Advanced economies have to contend with an infernal triptych resulting from deindustrialization and constituting obstacles to any decision to relocate. This triptych is characterized by : low skills levels in the workforce; higher wage costs (although the gap is no longer as wide as it was in the late 1990s, the hourly wage - including social security contributions - is still 20% higher, and 3.7 times more expensive than in Central and Eastern European countries (CEECs); the tax burden on companies (taken in the broadest sense, it represents 19% of GDP), which would require a threefold reduction in production taxes to bring the situation back into line (this tax burden is all the more worthy of questioning given that aid to companies also represents 8.4% of GDP; there is an urgent need to reflect on the coherence and complexity of a system that taxes in order to help).

We need to define a national strategy for rearming the production and commercial capacities of the company network. Gradually, some countries have moved away from a national focus on production. What was lost for 20 or 25 years was an ideological economic battle: a certain number of decision-makers simply considered that a company without a factory was preferable to a company with a factory. They'd just buy off the shelf, it was easier! In doing so, they overlooked an essential fact: when you lose a product, you don't just lose the product's current production and the jobs that go with it, you also lose the product's entire future and its entire history. You lose the research, the design, the marketing, and little by little, you let yourself be pushed out of the production groove.

While the negative impact of de-industrialization on foreign trade is now widely acknowledged, the content of the national strategy needed to remedy the situation is less clear-cut. Some experts have analyzed trade deficits in excess of $50 million. This analysis has guided the approach to reclaiming the productive base: several countries are world leaders in exporting agricultural products, but have serious deficits on other processed products from the same agri-food sector. Economists do not share the same vision, and place greater emphasis on competitiveness and winning back high-end production. As a result, this approach is not economically efficient. The aim is not to produce everything, but to specialize in high value-added sectors and define strategic products. Foreign trade figures illustrate a worrying situation, not in terms of values for a given year, but more in terms of the long-term trend of market and competitiveness losses.

It is essential to regain competitiveness in high-end, value-added manufacturing goods, to offset the energy deficit, which could continue to deteriorate with the ecological transition, particularly in the medium term. As far as supply vulnerabilities are concerned, it has to be said that a purely econometric approach leaves no room for common-sense criticism or for the political dimension that is so essential to understanding such a risk. First of all, it should be remembered that foreign supply for a given product does not in itself constitute a vulnerability, as long as this supply is not threatened by disruption or interruption. It has therefore developed an analysis grid to identify such risks. Around a quarter of exports correspond to foreign value-added (components, raw materials) that has been imported, processed and incorporated into exports. Another analysis takes the approach of applying filters to a country's imports according to certain vulnerability criteria to establish a list of vulnerable product categories. Both analyses consider imports from a majority of countries, and concentrated in a small number of countries, to be vulnerable. As a result, security strategies are focused on imported products, without any diversification of suppliers.

However, statistics are not detailed enough to know the origin of the components of a product imported locally, and therefore deemed non-vulnerable. For imports from third countries, we simply know the origin of the goods, but not the nationality of the company exporting from a third country. Nor for internal imports: it would be impossible to trace back the chain of origin for a good imported from China by one country and then exported to another. Thus, a good imported from a given economic area is not considered to be at risk, even though 90% of its components may come from countries such as China or Russia, or depend on a single imported component, as is the case with semiconductors. The semiconductor crisis has highlighted the very significant impact of a supply disruption concerning a single component. This risk of dependence is not surprising, given that over 50% of the global semiconductor market and 85% of semiconductors measuring less than 7 nanometres come from the same producer, Taiwan-based TSMC. In this case, it's clear that, even if German electric cars are statistically considered to be non-vulnerable imports for other European countries, their supply is nonetheless risky; this situation also raises the question of technological sovereignty.

Purely statistical vulnerability as it is understood today is therefore unreliable, and recent months have shown the repercussions of supply difficulties on the entire production chain. Moreover, relying on a purely econometric approach does not allow us to grasp all the supply risks a country may face. The Covid 19 crisis, for example, demonstrated that supply risks can exist outside the classic criteria of econometric vulnerability, and that certain know-how is vital to a country. The role of political leaders is therefore to anticipate possible scenarios and related strategies, by identifying supply risks that could have an impact on national security or sovereignty. Insufficient political appropriation of an economic risk has been noted in another area, that of debt. A number of economists put the foreign trade situation into perspective, explaining that, in any case, the current account deficit is smaller - though it still averaged $41.5 billion in 2020 - because it is somehow financed by net capital inflows: an average of $52 billion in 2020.

The current account balance covers trade in goods, trade in services, income flows and current transfers between advanced countries and the rest of the world. It is part of the balance of payments, which, by accounting definition, is always balanced. However, this current account balance is less deteriorated because U.S. companies have exported a lot of capital and produced a lot abroad. In addition, to finance the deficit, and since some of them are unable to sell, they are selling themselves. Their net foreign assets are becoming increasingly negative, averaging over $700 billion last year. It then reached 32.3% of GDP. The alarm has sounded! In this net foreign assets, you have $1,200 billion on average in public debt held abroad and $500 billion on average in net foreign surpluses from the private sector. This confirms that companies have clearly chosen to invest abroad to circumvent local production constraints. The fact that public debt is held by foreigners is not serious from a theoretical or economic point of view, even if some partners are annoyed by this situation, but it is not sustainable and cannot last.

The foreign trade strategy of certain countries is aimed at transforming the model used to support VSEs, SMEs and ETIs in exporting. The public policy of supporting companies is presented as one of three levels of action, alongside policies in favor of competitiveness and the articulation of export priorities at sector level. This reform has given rise to Team Export (TE), which brings together all the public solutions offered by the regions, government departments, chambers of commerce and industry, etc. to support local companies in their international expansion. With regional and international advisors, this network aims to offer effective assistance to local companies, notably via a one-stop shop. VSEs, SMEs and ETIs need to be able to draw on the support of an international advisor to help them prepare, plan and/or finance an international offering. This contact is the company's point of entry into the network of public export players. His or her role is to: enrich the portfolio of companies known to the TE network by contacting new prospects each year and qualifying their needs; direct companies in their portfolio towards certain free offers according to their needs; direct companies towards financial support if such is their need (in this case, the advisor passes on information about the company and its needs to the relevant territorial office, which then contacts the company); but above all, to sell international preparation and projection services, which can be implemented by the players. In the absence of such structures in certain countries, international chambers of commerce, private bodies under local law, are called upon to facilitate contacts and relations. We should also mention the work of foreign trade advisors and, of course, the regional economic departments of embassies.

In addition, regional agreements have been signed to make Team Export a tool at the service of regional economic development strategies, within the framework of the economic competence recognized by law. Local companies that have used TE's support services have welcomed the new organization and the government's desire to rationalize the intervention of public players. However, they regretted that the one-stop-shop process had not yet been completed, and that duplication still existed in some regions. They also pointed to a support offer that is largely unknown to companies, whose lack of export knowledge makes it difficult for them to take advantage of existing tools. Another criticism is the lack of information and database sharing between TE members. In parallel with the proposed aids and the territorial reorganization of public export players, a strategic export council has been set up, bringing together public and private players in foreign trade (organizations representing companies, private export support operators, etc.). The aim of this body is to formulate recommendations to the Managing Director and the Board of Directors, and to strengthen the coordination of export players at national and regional level.

Financial support for companies is diversified: direct government financing (Treasury loans, private sector study and assistance funds), export credits (export credit, international unsecured loans), public guarantees for foreign trade (export credit insurance, prospecting insurance), international corporate volunteering (VIE). On average, $225 million in loans are granted annually, $3.6 billion in outstanding balances on direct loans from the Treasury, and $245 million in public guarantees in 2021, for a total government expenditure on foreign trade support policy of around $800 million in 2021. It's worth pointing out the very positive results of the satisfaction surveys carried out among companies, and also describing in detail the range of export assistance available, particularly to VSEs, SMEs and ETIs. Some structures provide medium- and long-term credit insurance: this year, the volume averaged $17.3 billion, an increase of 37%, mainly due to the conclusion of major industrial contracts in the defense sector. Prospecting insurance rose by 23%: despite the sluggish health situation, our companies have adapted by digitizing their prospecting processes and maintaining a commercial link. Their territorial presence around the world has given them a form of agility where they are based, and prospecting has been able to continue. The volume of prospecting insurance business rose by 23%, mainly involving SMEs. Credit enhancement activities, i.e. international financing on the banking market, have not slowed down, with an 84% increase in export credit financing in 2021, a special type of engineering that makes a market reserved for large industrial companies accessible to many local SMEs.

It should be remembered, however, that without a global strategy, export subsidies will always be insufficient. As far as the national foreign trade strategy is concerned, we can say that the trade deficit is the result of an accumulation of local deficits: lack of competitiveness, lack of investment, lack of skills, lack of a structured strategy for each sector, lack of vision, lack of support. To this list must be added a more cultural, more psychological cause: exporting is a profession, a state of mind. It's a trade that has to be learned. And must be taught. Unfortunately, it has to be said that this assessment is still largely relevant, as the various public policies that have an impact on all the elements of competitiveness still seem to be steered in silos, without taking into account the challenges of foreign trade. A number of topics that appear to be disconnected from international trade issues, such as business transfers, skills and training, and corporate social responsibility, should be included in the national foreign trade strategy priorities, on a par with the policy of supporting companies in exporting. The approach to these issues should be much more systemic. The examples given here relating solely to countries' tax policies highlight the systemic effect of public policies and their impact on the development of these countries' foreign trade.

The annual analysis of foreign trade operators, often cited as an example of Team Export's performance, shows that in 2021, exports of local goods were carried out by an average of 136,400 companies (legal units). This number is up sharply on 2020 (+68,000 on average over one year). The concentration of the exporting apparatus is stable: the top 100 operators export 38% of the amounts in 2021, as in the previous year. ET representatives use this growth in the number of exporting companies to highlight the dynamism of their export support policy and their resilience to the health crisis. However, as was pointed out during the hearings, only 30% of first-time exporters export again the following year, and 25% export less than 5% of their sales. Moreover, this quantitative approach fails to address the essential issue of the development of mid-sized companies. Indeed, while some countries are no different from their neighbors in terms of the proportion of SMEs among exporting companies, they lag far behind in terms of the number of exporting ETIs. This weakness is not due to the export capacity of ETIs, but quite simply to their low numbers: 5,400 in France, 12,500 in Germany, 10,500 in the UK and over 8,000 in Italy. Although they represent only 4% of exporting companies, ETIs are responsible for 35% of export sales. They account for 25% of salaried employment, 34% of industrial jobs and 35% of international sales.

It should be noted that, from a customs point of view, there is a certain fragility among companies wishing to export, as they are more SMEs and VSEs. Like Germany, Italy boasts a network of highly specialized, export-oriented mid-sized companies, creating a veritable industrial fabric. This network of ETIs is an asset, particularly when it comes to acquiring market share, which is lacking in certain countries characterized by, on the one hand, very large groups and, on the other, a large majority of very small, undiversified companies. We need to develop the number of mid-sized companies in industry in these countries: in Germany, there are around 13,000 ETIs today, compared with around 5,300 in France. In Germany, this fabric of companies known as the Mittelstand accounts for 35% of total sales, and employs 60% of all employees and 82% of apprentices.

The scarcity of local medium-sized and intermediate companies can be attributed to the exorbitant taxation of inheritance. In Germany, companies stay in the family, whereas in France in particular, it's very complicated. French SMEs tend to be small, employing fewer than 10 people, which de facto leads to limited financial and human resources, unlike German SMEs. The analyses all converge on the same economic priority: to increase the number of ETIs. It should be remembered that 52% of SMBs are majority family-owned; if minority shareholdings are also taken into account, then 70% of SMBs in deficit countries like France are family-owned. Several studies converge to show that family shareholding is more conducive to long-term investment and hence innovation.

This makes the issue of family business transfers absolutely essential, given the urgent need for certain countries to revive their foreign trade. That's why it's so important to maintain the tax system that exempts 75% of transfers free of charge. This system, which has undergone several phases of modernization, only partially corrects the competitive disadvantage.

Yet the scheme is regularly attacked, notably in official government publications, while amendments tabled by Members of Parliament have attempted, fortunately in vain, to put an end to the scheme by way of an amendment to the Finance Bill. The priority of developing ETIs needs to be better asserted and supported, in particular through a genuine communication campaign aimed at company directors, 82% of whom are unaware of the existence of the scheme in their countries.

So it's not just the transfer tax that weighs on foreign trade. Historically, taxes on production have been much more unfavorable in some countries than in others. In 2018, taxes on production represented 3.6% of value added in some countries, compared with 0.5% in the leading countries. Since the early 2000s, due to the burden of taxation and administrative complexity, local companies have favored foreign investments over exports to expand internationally. Numerous testimonies have been gathered to illustrate this obstacle to business development, with, for example, a 3-year delay to obtain a building permit. Administrative complexity is compounded by a tendency not to support domestic companies in public procurement. In invitations to tender, the criterion of lowest cost almost always seems to take precedence over all others, whereas social or environmental considerations (such as carbon costs) or product quality could carry more weight.

All these obstacles have prompted managers to give priority to the development of subsidiaries abroad. With an average of 46,488 subsidiaries, advanced countries with an industrialization deficit have the most subsidiaries in the world, with a concentration on financial activities and manufacturing. The average outward flow of foreign direct investment (FDI) from these countries (1,364 billion in stock on average) is greater than the inflow of inward FDI (773 billion in stock). Above all, the weight of sales made by industrial subsidiaries abroad represents 2.5 to 3 times industrial value added. This strategy on the part of local companies is the direct result of a very different tax environment: high production taxes, capital taxes and inheritance taxes. These crucial issues do not seem to be on the agenda of strategic export councils.

These countries suffer from a lack of sector specialization because, unlike the United States and China, they have no direction. Who can say where industry in these countries will be in 10 or 20 years' time? The absence of vision is a real problem, because in these sectors, it's really long-term investment that produces results. The successes of German industry are the result of upstream thinking, and a very clear choice in favor of very high-end machine tools. In the absence of a clear direction, they try to make up for any difficulties as best they can. We also regret the lack of coordination between sectors and industries: the need to specifically support certain sectors and industries is important. However, until very recently, there was insufficient coordination between the national export strategy and the development priorities of the various industrial sectors. The decision to leave it up to companies to determine their export priorities has met with several limitations. The first of these relates to the very different levels of commitment of each sector to exports, and the second to insufficient coordination between these priorities and the action taken by the public authorities to support them. We would therefore have to criticize the lack of coordination between ET players, duplication and competition between public players, and the lack of coordination abroad.

It has to be said that the agendas of some of these bodies consisted of a simple round-table discussion of the players involved, summarizing their past and future activities. Despite their ambitious names, in recent years these bodies seem to have become essentially symbolic, with no real added value and falling far short of the objectives that may have been assigned to them. There is no pilot in the airplane, and there is no body that can address the challenges of foreign trade by involving the ministries and players whose actions are crucial to the competitiveness of local businesses. In several countries, the national strategy is limited to export assistance policies, without any consideration of the public policies that contribute to the competitiveness of local companies, or the challenges of reducing imports. This lack of strategic vision will be detrimental to the reindustrialization projects already announced, as it will not allow choices to be guided by real assets, nor by the needs most intrinsically linked to their sovereignty and independence. Finally, it is quite likely that decisions will be taken without first studying the feasibility of the projects, for example in terms of available skills.

When it comes to foreign trade, skills are crucial. First and foremost, the internationalization of companies must be based on specific skills: mastery of languages, knowledge and understanding of economic issues, reflexes that are indispensable to a company's internationalization projects, such as a good understanding of local culture and the needs of each country, etc. These skills cannot be improvised, and the company representatives interviewed deplored the lack of initial and continuing training. These skills cannot be improvised, and the company representatives we interviewed deplored the shortcomings of initial and continuing training. Moreover, public support for companies will never be able to compensate for the lack of culture and skills that are essential for innovation and export success. In terms of supply-side diversification, several countries are confronted with a lack of innovation on the part of local companies. Reducing margins to maintain price competitiveness has an impact on investment capacity, and therefore on innovation and internationalization. However, the search for supply-side diversification, and thus for comparative advantages, is not always a costly strategy, particularly as innovation can take many different forms. International trade skills can effectively take over from innovation: in this case, the aim is to adapt the production offer to the expectations of foreign markets, which is not very common in a culture that too often consists of proposing an offer that is too local. The Georges Monin group is a fine example of international success. The company began by targeting professionals, as it did not have the means to compete with mass retailers. To this end, it formed partnerships with cafés, brasseries and major players such as Pizza Hut and McDonald's. It has also developed an offer adapted to each country by proposing new flavors, as well as a range of services meeting the needs of bartenders around the world with local recipes. Between 75% and 80% of sales are now generated by exports.

The question of skills obviously goes beyond internal company issues, as it determines a country's non- price competitiveness. A country with high relative costs will tend to specialize in high-end, high-tech products. High-end and high-tech products require R&D and skills. And yet, the recovery plans of certain countries virtually ignore the question of education and, to a large extent, the fundamental issue of R&D. They are already lagging behind in these areas. Young people aren't doing enough science, and that's really what's at stake in the long term. You can't move upmarket if you don't have R&D and skills. When it comes to R&D (research and development), the gap between countries has been widening steadily. In 1996, the share of R&D expenditure was around 2.2% in France and Germany. In 2018, this rate was virtually unchanged in France, while in Germany it was 3.1%. Even at sector level, whether in the chemicals and pharmaceuticals or aeronautics industries, it can be seen that R&D investment intensity is higher in Germany. The French mistake of specializing in the mid-range is one of the reasons why France lags behind Germany.

Skills are also inextricably linked with the services sector, which is one of France's key foreign trade assets. In fact, unlike trade in goods, trade in services has generated a trade surplus for France over the last twenty years. Between 2000 and 2021, service exports grew by 142%, more than twice as fast as goods exports (+64%). Technological advances in information and telecommunications, greater outsourcing of service tasks by companies, and efforts to liberalize service sectors worldwide, have increased the amount of marketable activity beyond national borders. In 2018, there were 88,000 exporting companies, of which around 29,000 exported both goods and services. For every dollar these companies sell abroad, they sell 36 cents worth of services. These companies mainly belong to industrial sectors, in particular pharmaceuticals, where 66% of companies export both goods and services, and the manufacture of transport equipment, machinery and electrical equipment, where the rate is around 50%. A large proportion of the surplus in services can therefore be explained by the activity of companies classified as industrial, which are the real winners in international trade. Companies that export both goods and services are often twice the size of their competitors, generate 40% more added value and pay wages that are on average 25% higher.

This has two implications: if the industrial base were to shrink excessively, the capacity of local companies to export their services would also diminish; conversely, services are a gateway to reindustrialization, as in the case of Nervures, one of the world leaders in the paraglider market. Thanks to a partnership with the Applied Mathematics Department, Nervures has been able to develop new technologies and move upmarket with products for the French Ministry of Defence and Airbus. It has also been able to adapt during the health crisis, producing masks. But all this is only possible thanks to the development of skills. And yet, there is a not inconsiderable risk of telemigration, i.e. the flight of skills abroad and the consequent relocation of services. The above-mentioned lack of strategic vision is reflected in skills shortages, particularly in the service sector.

Some countries also have a singular propensity for over-transposing directives, particularly in the agricultural and agri-food sectors. I'm not saying that we should shy away from essential environmental and consumer protection considerations, but the evolution of trade balances in the agricultural and agri- food sectors is a flagrant demonstration of the fact that these countries have created constraints that their direct competitors do not have. The same applies to industry, where we are witnessing a piling-up of regulations and legislation, which has a direct impact on the efficiency of the local production system. Paradoxically, certain laws provide for numerous exemptions. In this way, the State itself is demonstrating that the common law system is penalizing! The overtransposition of extra legislation into local law is regularly denounced by companies, who feel that it places them at a competitive disadvantage by imposing burdens that other European companies do not have to bear. In the agricultural sector, the consequences of overtransposition and the absence of reciprocity with third countries are regularly denounced, as in the case of the ban on dimethoate for cherries produced in France, or the organic standards applying to bananas from the French West Indies.

This handicap is not only due to the tendency of certain countries to over-transpose their legislation, but also to the policy of imposing standards and rules on local companies that are not imposed on economic players in third countries, for example in the field of corporate social responsibility. In response to this self-fulfilling distortion of competition, it is important to ensure that the requirements for the publication of sustainability information are equivalent, in order to guarantee the competitiveness of companies in relation to their competitors. This would enable companies to compete on an equal footing. It would also appear that some organizations have over-transposed the plurilateral agreement on public procurement. Nearly 95% of contracts awarded within the European Union are covered by the agreement's stipulations, whereas only 32% of contracts in the United States, 28% in Japan and 16% in Canada are covered. The other non-EU countries (China, India, Russia, Brazil and Turkey) have not made any commitments, thus accentuating this distortion of reciprocity in terms of access to public procurement markets.

In addition, the trend in the use of trade defense instruments (anti-dumping and anti-subsidy measures) fell by almost 11% between 2000 and 2018, compared with an 82% increase in US measures over the same period. Some institutions over-transpose WTO multilateral rules, thereby depriving themselves of room for maneuver. The absence of mirror clauses is a real difficulty. The authorities in charge of the internal market and SMEs have suggested that the European Union has entered the era of the end of naivety, notably with the adoption of a new instrument designed to discourage discrimination against companies in the public procurement markets of third countries. The IPI (International Procurement Instrument) would enable public inquiries to be opened into allegations of discrimination against companies in public procurement. Should the existence of discriminatory restrictions on products, services and/or suppliers be established in the course of such an investigation, the country would be invited to consult on opening up its public procurement market. Following this mediation, and in the event of reciprocity being refused, the tool enables measures to be taken to limit access to open tenders for non-European companies from countries that do not offer similar conditions to their public procurement markets. The aim is therefore to encourage reciprocity in order to put an end to discrimination against companies in non-EU countries.

Integrating the cost of carbon into international trade will also be a decisive factor in restoring a better balance. In March 2022, an agreement was reached on the regulation establishing the Carbon Border Adjustment Mechanism (CBAM). The main aim of this environmental measure is to prevent carbon leakage, i.e. situations where locally-established companies might move their carbon-intensive production abroad to take advantage of lower standards, or where local products are replaced by more carbon-intensive imports. The aim is to encourage partner countries to implement carbon pricing policies to combat climate change. The MACF will be phased in gradually, and will initially apply only to a limited number of goods that present a high risk of carbon leakage, namely iron and steel, cement, fertilizers, aluminum and power generation. The MACF will only apply to the share of emissions that do not benefit from free allowances under the EU ETS (Emissions Trading Scheme), thus ensuring fair treatment of importers in relation to producers. The MACF will eventually replace the ETS.

In Germany, Italy and the UK, etc., it is possible to observe what made their export performance so successful, and what is appreciated in terms of company support. While Italy and, even more so, Germany are outperforming many of the industrialized countries of which they are the main partners, the UK will be recording a significant trade deficit in 2021 (around $150 billion, with a current account deficit of just $34 billion due to the surplus on services). The main lessons to be learnt are as follows: in Italy and Germany, price competitiveness has long outstripped that of local companies; tax systems encourage transfers, particularly family transfers; a strong culture of entrepreneurship among the population; and a genuine culture of hunting in packs to conquer foreign markets.

Large companies systematically involve the small and medium-sized businesses in their ecosystem in their export strategy. The local companies we interviewed all stressed this regrettable cultural difference, which penalizes them. Probably because of the industrial organization based mainly on large groups, it seems less natural for local companies to cooperate with their peers than in Germany or Italy. In Italy, cooperation is almost a necessity, since the productive organization of industrial districts is based on a strong division of labor and company specialization; a great respect for the value of work and a vocational training system that values apprenticeships and industrial trades; and a very strong organization of international trade fairs and shows: Germany leads Europe with a 50% market share, Italy is second with 23%, and France only 16%; in Germany, a banking culture of local, long-term support for companies; in Italy, an entrepreneurial culture that has long been geared towards the international arena, against the backdrop of a sluggish domestic market. In addition, Italy has provided substantial financial support for the post-health crisis recovery (+224% in financial aid between 2020 and 2021,

+58% in export credits). The ICE agency's support missions have become 95% free of charge, enabling Italian companies to take part in trade fairs abroad at no cost (the company pays only for transport and accommodation). The aid granted by the Italian government had created a real imbalance, and local companies were feeling the consequences; the UK has begun to implement a genuine data and economic intelligence strategy, based on the collection and use of sensitive company data, particularly from SMEs, to guide them as finely as possible towards export opportunities. The Ministry of Commerce said it was acting in a business logic within the ecosystem formed by public and private players, with a view to proposing a segmented approach to foreign markets. The aim is to change the situation in which 1 in 7 companies produces a good that could be exported, but does not do so.

As far as the proposals for a real public strategy are concerned, it has to be said that they highlight a cruel lack of strategic vision for turning around the foreign trade of advanced countries. The approach and thinking must absolutely be cross-functional, involving coordinated action by the various ministries that can influence the parameters of competitiveness (cost or non-cost). We urgently need to integrate objectives relating to the protection of sovereignty, and therefore independence from certain imports. The actions of ET players, whose work is appreciated in the field, are focused on developing exports, and not on the issue of imports. Yet reducing imports is clearly one of the levers not only for reducing the trade deficit, but also for building a national strategy to protect our sovereignty and independence. Relocation decisions can only succeed if the conditions for defining a global strategy are met. Such a strategy must take into account the new reality for these countries, namely the ecological transition. We need to project ourselves into a changing environment, where the rules will no longer be the same, for example in terms of transport.

That's why the first step is to pass an economic policy law, so that this strategy can be debated and adopted by the legislature. If it is to be effective, this strategy needs to set long-term objectives (at least 15 to 20 years) and identify the sectors, skills and companies to be supported. Within the strategic objectives, the question of services should be given particular attention, given the danger of telemigration, which will have a major impact on competitiveness in the years to come. Secondly, strategic export institutions need to be revamped, with governance better adapted to the real needs of foreign trade. All ministries in charge of public policies that have an impact on the competitiveness of local companies (taxation, national education, vocational training, research, etc.) must be involved.

As mentioned above, the transformation of SMEs into ETIs is one of the challenges for improving France's foreign trade performance. This development will also determine the success of future relocation and re-industrialization projects. This requires a legislative and regulatory framework that favors business transfers.

In addition, large local companies must be given greater incentives to hunt in packs to conquer foreign markets. A tax incentive and/or a specific label could help bring about this important cultural change. Given the lack of communication on export support measures for local companies, an information campaign should be organized on the support services offered to SMEs and ETIs by members of Team Export, and participation in international trade shows should be made free of charge for local companies, to take account of the competition from European companies, particularly Italian, at foreign trade fairs and shows.

Reinforcing language learning and knowledge of economics, mathematics, technology and international trade in secondary and higher education: this is the priority that needs to be included in the objectives of the ministries concerned, to ensure that skills useful to the competitiveness of local businesses do not remain an obstacle to the recovery of foreign trade. Another operational proposal concerns the tools to be made available to political decision-makers. The granularity of the data analyzed does not allow for a detailed analysis of the real supply risks. However, to support a long-term strategy of specialization in competitive sectors and relocation of production that contributes to economic sovereignty, we need to have all the relevant information at our disposal. It is therefore important to better assess the risks of supply vulnerability using customs data.

Another tool needs to be put in place, for the benefit of TE members, whose data sharing is not optimal. Inspired by the British experience, it would seem appropriate to propose the creation of a database that, with the help of artificial intelligence, would enable us to provide fine-tuned support to SMEs in their export activities. This database would be made up of free public data (open data) as well as studies carried out by private players, enabling us to identify opportunities in foreign markets. To this should be added the analysis of social networks, the content of which could be analyzed in real time by artificial intelligence (new trends, fashions, development of new technologies, etc.) to detect local needs likely to offer outlets for French production. Such a database could be managed by one of the members of the TE, who would then alert local companies capable of exporting the products or services thus identified. This whole process would, of course, have to be carried out within a framework defined by strict economic intelligence, ethical and legal rules.

.

Chapter 5

Comparative governance of reindustrialization mechanisms: towards applied business strategies

> The issue of foreign trade, and the trade deficit in particular, might seem insurmountable, given the catastrophic way in which the situation has evolved. This situation is the result of a strategic error: the choice, made by successive governments, of deindustrialization. Industry's share of GDP has fallen by 10 points since 1980, reaching 13.5% in 2019 in France, 24.2% in Germany, 19.6% in Italy and 15.8% in Spain. The ranking of these countries according to the share of industry in GDP is exactly the same as the ranking of the same countries according to their balance of trade.

This phenomenon of deindustrialization has been accompanied by numerous relocations. Local companies have relocated to produce more cheaply, thereby limiting the fall in purchasing power without necessarily conquering local markets. There are only 3.2 million industrial jobs in France, and 7 million in Germany. Logically, the decline in the number of industrial companies, which are more export-oriented than others, has led to a slowdown in industrial exports: between 2002 and 2020, they increased, in value terms, by just 1%-3.6%. You know the results of this deindustrialization. We mentioned them in the previous chapter, but it's worth recalling them briefly: the year 2021 was marked by a record deficit of $84.7 billion on average, compared with $64.7 billion in 2020 and $58 billion in 2019. That's an average deficit of $26.7 billion over two years. This accelerated deterioration, which could be attributed to the health crisis, is unfortunately not the first since 2002, the last year in which most of these countries had a positive trade balance. The deterioration continues in 2021, albeit at a slower pace than in 2020. This is partly due to an average $17.9 billion increase in the energy bill as a result of higher world energy prices. The figures for the first three quarters of 2022 already point to an average deficit of $149.9 billion.

We can emphasize the importance of the deficit in the energy sector for 2021. However, to consider that the balance of trade is mainly affected by the cost of energy imports is to ignore the real ills of deindustrialization. The consequences are equally disastrous when we compare one country with another. The figures from ExpertActions Group, whose calculation methods differ from those of the institutions, since they do not take into account trade movements within states, nevertheless offer a comparison that puts us at the bottom of the league. France is a long way behind Greece, Romania and Spain, with a 109 billion deficit! Let me remind you that France's three main customers are Germany, Italy and Belgium, all of which have a trade surplus. The deficit calculated by ExpertActions Group, shows the dependence of several countries on foreign trade; it is therefore not surprising to note that China is often their second largest supplier, averaging $63.8 billion, after Germany, with an average of $81.4 billion, and ahead of Italy, with an average of $46.3 billion. As we saw with the health crisis, this dependence raises the question of sovereignty, but we'll come back to that later.

The tragedy of de-industrialization, beyond the figures, can be seen on several levels. We must speak of the vicious circle brought about by deindustrialization: endemic unemployment, weakening of innovation and skills, weakening of the economy and reduced resistance of our country to shocks, such as a health crisis. The majority of advanced countries, including France, have to contend with an infernal triptych resulting from deindustrialization and constituting obstacles to any decision to relocate. This triptych is characterized by 1- low skills levels among the working population:

the OECD's Programme for International Assessment of Adult Competencies (PIAAC) survey on low skills levels among adults places France, for example, in 21ème position out of 24 countries surveyed; 2- high wage costs: although the gap with Germany is no longer as wide as it was at the end of the 1990s, the hourly wage - including social security contributions - is 20% higher than in the euro zone excluding France, and 3.7 times higher than in the Central and Eastern European countries (CEEC); Finally, the tax burden falls heavily on companies: taken in the broadest sense, it represents 19% of GDP, compared with 12% in the Eurozone. To bring France back into line with other European countries, production taxes would have to be cut by three times as much as the government has announced. It should be remembered that aid to businesses represents 8.4% of GDP, which makes us wonder about the coherence and complexity of a system that taxes in order to help. Simplification is a welcome way of tackling this situation.

To the "triptych" should be added the systematic use of debt. France's net international investment position, which reflects its indebtedness to the rest of the world, stands at 32.3% of GDP, close to the European warning threshold of 35%. This is a cause for concern, unlike the government, which prides itself on attracting foreign capital to buy and invest in France. Let's not forget the impact of Franco- European standards which, in the absence of controls, do not apply to imports that compete with our own production. Take, for example, the ban on dimethoate for cherries produced in France, the animal welfare requirements for our chickens, or the organic standards applying to bananas from the French West Indies.

Finally, it should be pointed out that the difficulty of the subject we have dealt with lies in the fact that there is no miracle solution, no flagship measure that will solve a large part of the problem. Indeed, the balance of trade is the result of a number of public policies that are all too often thought of in silos: taxation, research and innovation, training and skills enhancement, and so on. Any approach must therefore be cross-functional and ecosystemic. However, it has been confirmed that the export support policy does not follow any strategy, neither sectoral nor geographical outside Africa; just like the recovery and reindustrialization policy, which responds to projects without any sectoral strategy. Rebalancing the trade balance will be achieved by accelerating exports, but also by reducing imports.

What are the multitudes of risks and public policies that have an impact on foreign trade? Indeed, cross- functionality and the definition of a strategy are essential, given the diversity of the risks involved, which means that the objective of foreign trade must be considered through the prism of numerous public policies. The issue of services in particular illustrates this necessity. While the balance of trade in goods is alarming, it needs to be qualified by the performance of the services sector, which is in surplus. This level is even very high in 2021, with a positive balance of $36.2 billion. In addition to tourism, of course, this figure is mainly attributable to transport services, in particular shipping companies, but also to business services, technical services, professional services and management consulting services.

Between 2000 and 2021, service exports grew by 140%, or twice as much as goods exports, and rose from 24% to 33% of total exports. The share of services is therefore increasing significantly. What's more, in 2021, service exports accounted for 25% of France's current account credits, compared with 16% for Germany and 13% for Italy. As a result, our weakness in goods is partly offset by our surplus in services. The predominance of services in the French economy can also be seen in our investments abroad. In fact, they account for 55% of the total stock of investments, compared with 36% for industry and manufacturing.

The question of services must be central to our approach to foreign trade, firstly because the good performance of services in terms of exports offsets the very heavy deficit in the goods trade balance, with, in addition, the primary income surplus, which amounted to $81 billion to achieve a current account balance slightly in surplus, to the tune of $9 billion in 2021. So, overall, we can say that things aren't too bad for 2021, since the current account balance is in surplus. But over the last 10 years, it has only been in surplus for 2 years, and it will once again be in very large deficit in 2022. But services are above all essential because they are intrinsically linked to exported goods, often complementing them. In fact, 40% of the value added incorporated into goods exports is actually made up of services.

Many companies export both goods and services, particularly in the industrial sector. In the pharmaceuticals sector, for example, 66% of companies export both goods and services. Companies that export both goods and services are generally twice the size of their competitors. They generate 40% more added value and pay wages that are on average 25% higher. If the industrial base were to shrink excessively, of course the ability of companies to export services would also shrink significantly. So just because we have a surplus in services doesn't mean we should neglect the balance of trade. The relocation of services also represents a risk, particularly with the development of digital technologies. As we shall see later, training is essential, as is investment in digital infrastructures.

While we often hear of highly qualified people supporting cutting-edge research projects developed in France, this is less true of the majority. Expert reports on skills highlight the insufficient level of skills available, and the negative impact on France's non-price competitiveness. Indeed, the benefits of innovation and robotization in industry are limited by the lack of skills in the workforce. European Investment Bank, OECD: all studies have been sounding the alarm on this subject for some time. It represents a real challenge for foreign trade. By neglecting this public training policy, France could be confronted with the phenomenon of tele-migration in favor of workers from developing countries, as described by the economist Richard Baldwin. This is why the fight against offshoring must include a services strategy.

Another risk is that of intellectual property, in particular, due to dependence on data centers located abroad. We now know, after sometimes painful experiences, that even if our companies think they have complete ownership and control of their data, this is not the case. In fact, even when it comes to goods, the risk of dependency is underestimated. This has already been mentioned.

In fact, some countries have a poor understanding of their true vulnerabilities, due to insufficient precision in the origin of goods imported and accounted for by the customs department. This dimension is often neglected in thinking about foreign trade and in the definition of public policies in France. The same applies to competition. Obviously, the notions of price and non-price competitiveness are always recalled, but without all the consequences being drawn. This is particularly true of non-price competitiveness, which depends on a number of factors, including the normative environment, and positioning - we have seen, for example, that France has abandoned the top end of the market in sectors such as the automotive industry. It also depends on the characteristics of exporting companies, their size, their management, and other structural factors such as qualifications, skills or R&D.

In all these respects, the feeling is that there is no strategic direction for France. The question of planning seems essential. Training still seems too disconnected from skills needs, which makes it difficult to conceive of a new, more upmarket positioning for many products, as in Germany, for example. Our expert reports on business transfers have also shown that certain countries are sorely lacking in ETIs, the majority of which are family-owned, and that the tax and legislative framework, instead of facilitating the development of these export champions, constrains them. In this respect, there is an essential difference with Germany and Italy, which partly explains the weakness of foreign trade in several countries, including France. There are even strong temptations to call into question the mechanisms that support them, even though the 5,400 French ETIs alone account for 34% of our exports! Moreover, there seems to be a French obsession with the number of companies that export. The country focuses on the number of exporting companies, even if it means giving priority to helping small, first-time exporters who, in reality, don't have much potential. Instead, it should focus on supporting companies that can achieve significant sales abroad. What's more, Business France's business model encourages its staff to spend more time on paid commercial missions, such as VIEs (International corporate volunteering) - which account for a significant proportion of Business France's revenue - rather than focusing on free advice for the benefit of those companies best equipped to go international. As we can see, this is not a winning model, as is the case in Italy. Business France's counterpart agency, ICE, offers free support, such as free participation in trade fairs abroad. In short, the situation is one of support for SMEs and ETIs that follows no logic, no strategy that is truly favorable to foreign trade in the long term.

Another neglected issue is that of competition with third-country companies, which all too often seems not to be an issue for public purchasers, who give preference to the lowest bidder, to the detriment of companies, even though the Ministry of the Economy and Finance has pointed out that public procurement law allows the use of bid selection criteria such as the development of direct sourcing, performance in terms of environmental protection, in particular the ecological impact of transporting supplies or personnel, or a service provider's response times if justified by the purpose of the public contract. Our European neighbors, on the other hand, do not hesitate to support their national companies.

Finally, international competition does not seem to be sufficiently anticipated and taken into account in national assessments of the impact of European decisions. CSR reporting obligations will place a heavier burden on European SMEs. What's more, the European Union makes almost no use of trade defense instruments, whereas the United States makes massive use of them. We often have the impression that Europe shoots itself in the foot and never, or at least very inadequately, sets the conditions for reciprocity with third countries. As you can see, some countries are still a long way from realizing the impact of decisions on non-price competitiveness. And this can be felt in the way SMEs and SMIs are supported in their international expansion. There is no miracle solution, but a new strategy needs to be defined.

While there is no miracle solution for redressing the balance of trade and making small and medium- sized businesses more competitive, there is a collective obligation to define and implement a genuine foreign trade strategy. This is the common thread running through our proposals, which are structured around strategic and operational objectives. First of all, it should be recalled that the Strategic export consulting, CSE, and the Team Export, TE, exist and represent undeniable progress since the reform resulting from the so-called Roubaix strategy, presented in 2018. However, there is a lack of long-term strategy for France, and a need to strengthen the governance of Team Export.

Proposal no. 1 therefore aims to define a long-term strategy for France's foreign trade, at the very least up to 2040, in order to define the objectives - particularly in terms of economic sovereignty - and identify the key sectors and skills to be supported. The definition of this strategy is a matter for both Government and Parliament, and could be based on an economic orientation law for France. The terrible consequences of past strategic choices have been demonstrated, as has the absolute necessity of thinking about foreign trade in an ecosystemic way. The executive and legislative powers must now assume the eminently political role of guiding global foreign trade policy, which concerns both imports and exports.

This proposal aims to renew the governance of the Strategic export consulting (CSE), in order to effectively steer the national strategy defined in advance by integrating foreign trade objectives into the various public policies that have an impact on the balance of goods and services, while ensuring effective coordination between these policies. The renewed CSE should move beyond the confines of Business France, where it advises the Board of Directors, and become an interministerial body, as well as a multisectoral one, coordinating public and private players. The draft resolution could recommend requesting an annual report on the balance of trade, tracking not only exports but also imports.

A logical extension of the previous proposals, the third concerns Team Export, which must translate strategic orientations into action in the field and with VSEs, SMEs and ETIs with real international potential. The unity of action between the various components of the TFE must be strengthened, and the results of its action in the territories formally presented to the Strategic export consulting.

The fourth and final recommendation under the strategic objectives is to better integrate the issue of services into the fight against offshoring. This proposal might seem redundant with the previous ones, insofar as it should logically follow on from them. However, the lesson of the strategic error of de- industrialization leads us to insist on the services dimension, which today constitutes an asset for economically advanced countries, but also a significant risk if nothing is done to preserve its strength. This objective therefore focuses on training, skills and digital infrastructures in the regions, as tools in the fight against relocation.

In terms of operational objectives, the proposal concerns relocation and reindustrialization, by facilitating business transfers and supporting SMEs and ETIs. It will be implemented in particular through the draft law which will take up all the proposals. Proposal no. 6 aims to encourage companies to hunt in packs, since this is one of the major weaknesses of French culture when it comes to conquering foreign markets. This incentive could be based on a targeted tax system and/or the promotion of a specific Made in France label for export. Proposal no. 7 aims to organize an information campaign on the support services offered to SMEs and ETIs by Team Export. It also aims to draw inspiration from the Italian example by making participation in international trade fairs free of charge for local companies.

Because the importance of skills in non-price competitiveness cannot be stressed enough, proposal no. 8 aims to reinforce language learning and knowledge of economics, mathematics, technology and international trade in secondary and higher education. Proposal no. 9 focuses on supply vulnerabilities, which need to be better identified using customs data that the European Commission could make available to countries.

Lastly, proposal no. 10 aims to define the content, framework and ethical rules for the creation and operation of a French database which, with the help of artificial intelligence, will enable us to provide fine-tuned export support for SMEs. Such a database would be made up of public data (open data), paid-for data (including studies carried out by consultants), data from the companies themselves, as well as information from social networks, whose activity could be studied using artificial intelligence, and put to good use in guiding companies towards export markets in near-real time. This proposal echoes the database project currently underway at the UK Department for International Trade, which regrets the lack of sharing of useful information between Team Export members. The management of this database could be entrusted to a member of the TFE, in compliance with economic intelligence rules.

Great Britain, now outside the European Union, also has a structural trade deficit in goods, representing 6.7% of its GDP, i.e. a deficit of $185 billion, but a trade balance in services with a large surplus of $150 billion. Including services, the deficit is £29 billion in 2021, or $34 billion. As the deficit structure is similar to that of France, it was interesting to understand how British players are approaching the challenge of foreign trade, particularly in a very particular context that has forced them to endure both the effects of the health crisis and those of Brexit, with the negotiation of new trade terms.

In 2020 and 2021, the United Kingdom saw a sharp contraction in its trade with the European Union, which nevertheless remains its leading trading partner. This is also true for France, whose balance of goods with the UK, while remaining in surplus, fell from $9.8 billion to $6.9 billion. France is the UK's fifth-largest customer, and only seventh-largest supplier. The UK has specialized in the export of services. It has fully assumed this position. Re-industrialization is meaningless without pure comparative advantages, and a deficit is not in itself a handicap for the British. Their sole objective is to ensure that supplies are maintained, whatever the supplier. Economic dependence for certain goods is therefore not structurally problematic.

British pragmatism has to be emphasized. First of all, in terms of trade strategy, the country has turned to partners other than European ones to seal agreements after leaving the European Union. A free trade agreement was signed with Australia in

December 2021. Although the expected direct economic benefits appear minimal for the moment (0.08% of GDP in 2035), the UK considers that this agreement will enhance its access to the Trans-Pacific Partnership, which brings together eleven countries, including Vietnam, Canada, Japan and Malaysia.

The UK government has begun a review of the arrangements to help businesses internationalize. In January 2018, it launched a consultation that includes export and investment promotion, non-tariff barriers and entrepreneurs' attitudes to international trade. This reflection is part of the Global Britain project, the international side of the EU withdrawal process, which refers to the UK's post-Brexit foreign and trade policy priorities. The Department for International Trade has stepped up its contacts with OECD countries, including at ministerial level, and created a bimonthly forum bringing together heads of economic missions in London to promote its reforms and exchange best practices. Somewhat neglected in recent years, the policy of supporting exports and promoting investment could therefore evolve significantly on the occasion of this reflection, which has not yet fully come to fruition due to the Brexit and the health crisis, which have fully mobilized the British authorities for the past three years.

In the UK, the Department for International Trade (DIT), which absorbed the former UK Trade & Investment (UKTI) agency, is responsible for export support and investment promotion. With a staff of around 4,400 and an annual budget of over £696.5 million, the DIT offers a range of progressive services, including a dedicated package for companies bidding for contracts worth over £250 million. Following the example of Business France's transformation, the DIT has been working for several years with chambers of commerce in France's regions and abroad. Last autumn, the government announced the creation of an interdepartmental working group under the authority of the DIT, the Office for Investment. Its mission is to stimulate foreign investment in priority sectors: carbon neutrality, infrastructure, R&D. The government had indicated that this unit would be made up of highly experienced individuals, with experience in both the private sector and public administrations, and would be tasked, among other things, with helping to remove potential barriers (regulatory constraints, planning problems, etc.) to the realization of first-rate investments.

Export support and investment promotion are now handled exclusively by the Global Trade and Investment Directorate (GTI) within the DIT. For the period 2020-20220, the GTI had an annual budget of
£207.4 million. The DIT offers a number of evolving services. Formerly free of charge, the majority of the DIT's export support products are now subject to a fee, in order to make an initial selection among candidate companies. These services are built around three flagship products: the Growth Gateway and the Overseas Market Introduction Service, which can be supplemented by various communication and networking services. DIT also offers an original product, the High Value Opportunities programme (HVO), which is reserved for companies bidding for tenders worth over £250 million, mainly in the construction sector. The HVO is run by a GTI unit that identifies tenders, contacts British companies and lobbies foreign contractors.

DIT is present in 113 countries and employs over 1,460 people overseas. Through the British diplomatic network, which includes over 80 embassies and 35 consulates offices, DIT is present in a total of 113 countries. It is supported by the international network of the British Chambers of Commerce. This architecture allows a certain flexibility in the way services are delivered, with the same pricing structure but a variety of different forms. In addition, it creates synergies between the DIT, the BCCs and the 38 Local Enterprise Partnerships, which are sometimes associated with the Chambers' activities, particularly in promoting foreign investment. A large proportion of DIT's regional services are provided by private partners. The DIT's regional offices are staffed by 350 export advisors, with only a few dozen permanent staff responsible for management functions. With the exception of the London region, most contract staff come from the 53 British Chambers of Commerce (BCC).

In some countries, services for SMEs have been delegated to chambers of commerce, which have long complained of unfair competition from DIT, particularly in China. Today, BCCs provide coaching, accommodation, discovery and prospecting services on behalf of DIT in over twenty markets. Financial support from the DIT cannot exceed 20% of the cost of the services provided by the chambers. Once delegated, DIT teams concentrate on major contracts and strategic relationships, while ensuring that the quality and price of delegated services are maintained. This partnership should eventually extend to other countries, thanks to DIT's capacity-building initiatives aimed at federating existing business associations, along the lines of the German experience in West Africa.

Digital technology is playing an increasingly important role in the DIT's strategy, and all public platforms for exporters have been merged onto the great.gov.uk website. In addition to providing a clearer offering, this one-stop shop offers a more efficient service thanks to interactive tools that inform inexperienced entrepreneurs about export opportunities and the steps to take. It also helps export advisors to identify companies likely to be interested in export support. In addition, DIT has set up a program to promote e-commerce by offering discounted access to several online sales sites, including Amazon and eBay. The DIT also recruited a Chief Technological Officer in 2018 to define an IT strategy for the department, develop a digital culture, and ensure the provision of IT services for exporting companies. Lastly, the DIT offers exporters the opportunity to sign up to a mailing list enabling them to be alerted in real time to foreign tenders. In 2020-2021, the budget allocated to the DIT is £39 million.

The DIT network is organized around nine overseas Trade Commissioners. The Trade Commissioners work closely with British Ambassadors and High Commissioners (based in Commonwealth countries), the diplomatic network and administrations based in the countries in their region, and are responsible for stimulating exports and imports with their region, as well as promoting the government's trade policy. The creation of these nine geographical zones is intended to go hand in hand with the adoption of a bottom-up approach, enabling greater attention to be paid to the specific features of the markets under consideration, since DIT strategy can vary from one zone to another. In addition, these 9 commissioners are now placed under the authority of the Foreign Commonwealth Office, which has also merged with the Department for International Development, to enable greater integration and coherence between foreign policy and trade and development policy.

The Director General for Exports at the Department for International Trade presented the impressive data and business intelligence strategy being implemented. A process for collecting and using confidential data from all British companies has been put in place, with the aim of guiding each SME more precisely towards the most relevant foreign markets. In this way, the government is taking a business approach to the ecosystem formed by all public and private players. Only by having access to the most detailed information on SMEs can we offer a segmented, individualized approach to markets, targeting opportunities that correspond to the diversity of each company. Today, one in seven companies produces a good that could be exported, but does not do so. These companies are targeted by the Ministry of Foreign Trade. This data strategy complements financial support schemes for exports, such as UK Export Finance, which manages public export guarantees.

As far as a dynamic credit insurance policy is concerned, in the UK, public export guarantees have been managed since 1919 by UK Export Finance (UKEF), which offers a wide range of products, including a direct lending facility. The agency has an operating budget of around £285 million and a staff of 403. It is fully responsible for public export guarantees, excluding development aid, and mainly supports SMEs (79% of aid granted in 2020-21). Aid granted by UKEF must not exceed a credit risk exposure of £50 billion. This ceiling is set for each country, and may be as high as £5 billion. The credit risk exposure for a given market may nevertheless exceed the initial ceiling if the Treasury gives its approval. In the 2020-21 financial year, UKEF granted a total of £12 billion in aid, almost three times as much as the previous year's figure of £4.4 billion.

In total, UKEF has helped 549 businesses, employing almost 107,000 people in the UK. UKEF's portfolio for 2020-21 is as follows: 52.1% of credit exposure for industry; 13% for specialist, scientific and technical activities; 11.2% for retail and mass distribution; and 6.5% for construction. Overall, and according to the British Exporters Association's 2019-2020 rankings, UKEF's range of products to help companies export is the best in Europe (score of 9/10), although it does not include currency hedging.

As far as Italy is concerned, it has to be said that in 2021, Italy's coverage rate has continued to rise to 116.6% (after 112.6% in 2019) and, excluding energy, even reaches 125.4%. Italy moved up one place to become the world's 8e exporter (2.9% of world exports in 2020) and the 3ème European exporter, after Germany (7.9%) and the Netherlands (3.9%), ahead of France (2.8%). Italy moves up two places to become 11ème world importer (2.4% of world imports); behind Germany (6.7% share), the Netherlands (3.4%) and France (3.3%).

Italy is France's third-largest trading partner and its third-largest trade deficit. France is the third-largest destination for Italian subsidiaries. More than half of these investments are in the manufacturing sector.

Italy has holdings in over 2,000 French companies, representing more than 100,000 jobs. France's stock of direct investment is twice that of Italy. France's trade balance with Italy was in deficit to the tune of

13.3 billion in 2020, down on 2019 due to the COVID crisis (15.7 billion). An essential lever for the Italian economy (30% of GDP), exports enjoy a strong political consensus. Successive governments have always paid particular attention to this sector, providing significant resources for support policies and promoting trade diplomacy and free-trade agreements.

Italy, which by 2021 has reached its target of exceeding $500 billion in export volume ($516 billion, with exports up +18.2% on 2019), does not think in terms of trade balance, but in terms of volume, the number of regular exporting companies (stable at 90,000 out of 137,000, according to Confindustria) and market share. Rather than grouping together companies from the same sector (industrial districts), it is now the sectors that receive the most support, with multi-level representation. The entire value chain behind the product is thus supported. The excellence of the transalpine economy is based on its manufacturing industry. Exports of services are not a priority. The priority sectors (in terms of their contribution to GDP) are mechanical engineering (30%), fashion (17%) and agri-food (15-20%). North- South dualism is also reflected in foreign trade results: the 8 southern regions export less than 10% of the total. Exports from these regions are mainly agri-food.

Italy's success in foreign trade is due to a strong political will that recognizes this major asset for the entire transalpine economy. There are many players involved in export financing, and several public entities are involved: the Cash deposits loans (CDP, under the supervision of the Ministry of the Economy and Finance) finances (generally in co-financing with banks) directly or refinances major contracts of over $25 million; SIMEST (a subsidiary of CDP, under the supervision of the Ministry of Foreign Affairs) finances (soft loans) exports and foreign investment (minority stakes in the capital of joint ventures abroad); the public insurer SACE (controlled by the MEF since March 22, 2022) guarantees export operations; the regions (shared competence) financially support their companies (between $80 and $120 million per year); Invitalia (controlled by the Ministry of Economic Development) grants subsidies to SMEs for digitization for internationalization purposes.

The Finance Act sets the budget dedicated to export support over 3 years (which changes with each Finance Act). Since January 1er 2020, the competences and part of the dedicated staff of the Ministry of Economic Development have been transferred to the Ministry of Foreign Affairs and International Cooperation - MAECI (Directorate for the Promotion of the Sistema Paese), as have the supervision of the ICE agency and the credits for the promotion of foreign trade. Trade policy was transferred to the European Union

Directorate, and support for business internationalization to the General Directorate for the Promotion of the Sistema Paese (country system). Chambers of Commerce, including those abroad, remain the responsibility of the Ministry of Economic Development.

The Italian Trade Agency (ITA, or ICE), an organization under the supervision of MAECI, is responsible for promoting "Made in Italy" abroad and attracting investment to Italy. It has 500 employees in Italy and 120 expatriates abroad, to which must be added 500 employees on local contracts. It has an annual promotional budget of $170 million and an operating budget of $130 million (not fungible). Its overseas network has been reduced and integrated into the embassies. Since the Covid-19 crisis, 95% of ICE's activities have become free of charge (i.e., financed from the agency's budget), including participation in trade shows abroad (companies pay only for accommodation and transport). There are no restrictions on the number of participants or on company size. Agreements have been signed with digital platforms (33) and universities.

ICE prepares the three-year strategy, which is then adopted by an inter-ministerial committee (cabina di regia) that brings together the relevant ministries, stakeholders and the State-Regions conference once a year (at the end of the year) to adopt operational conclusions for the year ahead. ICE's role in export support was strengthened during the crisis, notably by centralizing the competence previously devolved to the CCIs, which were often small and comparable to mere business clubs, and ICE now centralizes all actions. The regions, which share responsibility for foreign trade with the State, are generally very active in supporting exports, notably through institutional missions, participation in international trade fairs, organization of events and seminars, and financial support for companies. Our proactive foreign trade support policy is based on six pillars:

A major promotional campaign from December 2021 to August 2022, "Italy is simply extraordinary: beIT", worth $104 million, which has had a very strong impact, particularly on social networks;

Enhanced training a with the creation of the smart export academy, which offers 10,000 enrolees online courses with Italy's leading universities and business schools. Diplomatic staff are trained in the tools by the various operators;

An export.gov.it one-stop shop launched in September 2020, bringing together the training and information tools of the MAE, ICE, Sace, Simest, CCI and Regions, and registering more than 85,000 users in February 2022;

Public support for the digitization of e-commerce: 2,200 SMEs have benefited from a $20,000 subsidy for the employment of a "digital temporary export manager" and 7,000 micro-enterprises (fewer than 10 employees) from a $4,000 subsidy for investments linked to digitization and e-commerce. 32 contracts have been signed in 2020-2021 with international platforms for the creation of "Made in Italy" showcases, including Amazon, Alibaba, WeChat, Flipkart and Walmart, and 4,000 companies have taken part in initiatives with large retailers abroad. 4,520 companies were admitted to e-commerce platforms promoted by ICE (7,376 over the 2019-21 period);

Expertise in trade show organization. Italy is Europe's second-largest trade fair market, after Germany. According to the industry association AEFI, every year 50% of exports are the result of contacts made at trade fairs;

Massive public financing of exports. The 2022 Finance Act allocates $1.5 billion to the revolving fund ($1.2 billion for SIMEST) and $150 million to the integrated promotion fund (Ministry of Foreign Affairs) for subsidies (conversion of part of the SIMEST subsidized loans into grants). This public funding concerns : equity investments: $143 million(+64%), including $36 million from subsidized rates and $43 million from the venture capital fund. 100 million was allocated to refinance the venture capital fund managed by Simest, bringing the total endowment to $160 million. Simest takes minority stakes in the capital of early-stage startups (up to 49%). An agreement has been signed with CDP Venture (national innovation fund) to identify startups with internationalization needs; over 5 billion in export credits (+58%), including 4.6 billion in buyer credits and 406 million in supplier credits; a high-performance $27 billion insurance system to support the internationalization of companies, which is estimated to have generated $13.8 billion in additional sales and created or maintained over 40,000 jobs in 2019, with 75% of the beneficiaries of this fast-growing insurance (500 in 2018 to over 1,300 in 2019) being SMEs. Machine tools account for 30% of the number of operations, which has doubled in ten years (from 1,000 in 2008 to 2,000 in 2019), particularly those for the fashion, construction and agri-food sectors. The other main beneficiaries are the technology-intensive and transportation sectors.

Overall, from 2010 to 2019, the number of exporting companies in Italy rose by 3.4%. Italy places great emphasis on training entrepreneurs to export, and is particularly agile in helping its companies weather crises and conquer new markets. During the COVID crisis, Italy's National Recovery and Resilience Plan (NRRP) was put in place, with $68.9 billion in grants and $122.6 billion in loans under the Recovery and Resilience Facility (RRF). The plan included the refinancing of the SIMEST-managed export aid fund to the tune of $1.2 billion, 40% of which was earmarked for companies in the Mezzogiorno. SIMEST had to double its staff to be able to respond to financing requests targeting the digital and ecological transition, the commercial development of SMEs abroad and participation in trade fairs and exhibitions abroad.

In the summer of 2021, Italy opened its first Italian innovation and culture hub (IICH) in California's Silicon Valley. The center, which brings together the cultural institute, the ICE for investment attraction and the innovation center, aims to promote Italian technological products. If successful, the initiative will be replicated in other countries.

In the case of Germany, even though in May 2022, for the first time since 1991, the country's trade balance widened, leaving some commentators to speak of a model on its last legs, it has nonetheless recorded surpluses averaging around $10 billion a month since 2000. Unlike France, it is therefore able to absorb shocks. In 2021, foreign trade surpluses still contributed over 5% to German economic growth. The new difficulties are therefore more a test of the German economy's ability to bounce back.

In 2021, with a total trade volume of $164 billion (+12% on the previous year), Germany remained by far France's biggest trading partner, its biggest customer ($62 billion in imports from France, up 11%) and its biggest supplier ($102 billion in exports to France, up 12%). The 4,500 or so German companies operating in France employ 325,000 people, representing a considerable economic weight. Also in 2021, Germany was the leading investor in France, both in Europe and worldwide, overtaking the United States. 5,700 French companies are present in Germany, where they have created over 400,000 jobs and generated sales of $86 billion. Germany's trade slowed sharply in 2020 compared with 2019. China consolidates its position as Germany's leading trading partner. Germany's trade surplus deteriorates, due in particular to a sharp decline in automotive and machinery exports. In the specific context of the health crisis and its differentiated economic impacts, trade with France declines. While France remains Germany's fourth-largest trading partner, Poland is now Germany's fourth-largest supplier.

Despite a highly favorable system, Germany is facing a problem of company transfers, not least for demographic reasons. One in eight managers will soon be retiring in Germany. As in France, there is a severe shortage of skilled workers, particularly in the care, gastronomy, engineering and IT sectors. Some Länder, such as North Rhine-Westphalia, are home to long-established heavy industry (coal and steel). These need to be supported in their transformation.

We need to highlight a system that is not necessarily more fragmented. It could be more, given Germany's federal tradition. Three factors may explain its strength: the resources allocated are greater than those observed elsewhere; the division of tasks is perhaps clearer between players accustomed to a decomposition of decision-making in Germany, with coordination processes that are perhaps more regular; an economic structure geared towards industry and exports, accustomed to the pooling of certain information and to regular exchanges between its players, notably thanks to the network of chambers of commerce. Nevertheless, the tools developed seem to be coming up against the need to adapt a German model that is losing momentum in the face of increasing international competition and the development of new modes of production and internationalization (digital, platforms, e-commerce). Here, the investment guarantee scheme meets a need to secure investments by German companies abroad. Investment guarantees have been used for decades by the German government to promote German foreign investment. The aim is to support German companies wishing to invest in promising foreign markets, by removing certain extreme political risks. The principle is relatively straightforward: investment guarantees insure companies' investments against political risks in target countries; these investments in turn boost growth and employment in Germany.

In 2018, $1.2 billion in state guarantees were granted to German companies. Demand from companies was much higher ($3.97 billion). In 2018, total guaranteed investments amounted to $33.8 billion. Projects benefiting from investment protection led to investments of $3.3 billion worldwide. 26% of users are new, reflecting the dynamism of the scheme. The operation of the guarantee is slightly flexible in terms of coverage (equity, quasi-equity, etc.) and beneficiary (bank, company, etc.). In all, these investment guarantees have financed 51 projects in 17 countries; 37% of accepted projects were implemented by SMEs. 96% of companies that have used these schemes claim to have saved jobs, and 90% to have created new ones in Germany. 11,500 jobs were created in investment countries. Overall, 96% of companies that benefited from the scheme said they were satisfied.

To obtain this guarantee, sufficient legal protection in the host country, such as the signing of a bilateral investment protection agreement or a similar agreement between the country in question and the European Union, is normally required.

The decision as to whether or not to finance a particular project is taken by an inter-ministerial committee, but PwC -

PricewaterhouseCoopers GmbH - the auditing firm delegated with the operational management of the scheme, also has a say. In reality, investment security is not just a matter of financial insurance. The German government uses other, more political and diplomatic tools to encourage direct investment abroad, with the aim of reducing risks in host countries through a policy of guaranteeing direct investors abroad. Germany also has a system of financing guarantees designed to facilitate the supply of strategic raw materials to German companies ($3.8 billion in outstandings).

Germany has put in place an extensive export support network. The Federal Ministry of Economics and Energy (BMWi) contributes to the support of organizations in charge of export promotion and attractiveness. In 2021, the total budget for the federal government's support system for export- oriented companies (excluding tourism promotion and participation in the budgets of international organizations) was $733.5 million, representing a major increase (3.5-fold). However, this increase can be explained by the adoption of a specific strategy for international cooperation in hydrogen (which alone accounts for $390 million). The remaining sums are allocated to promoting foreign trade through two bodies, described below, and up to 45.1 million to organizing German pavilions at trade fairs abroad. This sum is administered by BAFA, an agency of the Federal Ministry of Economics, in conjunction with AUMA, the German Trade Fair Association. In addition, there is 8 million in specific support for SMEs and

2.5 million for young innovative companies - figures that are stable compared to 2020 - and credits for specific actions.

In addition to subsidies at federal level, many Länder also have their own support schemes for internationalization, for example in North Rhine-Westphalia with NRW Invest and NRW International, responsible respectively for investment promotion and support for the internationalization of companies. The largest budgets are generally devoted to promoting the attractiveness of the Länder concerned. In addition to North Rhine-Westphalia, Bavaria and Baden-Württemberg are among the Länder that devote substantial funding to the internationalization of their companies. At regional level, German SMEs can also take advantage of a range of financial products set up by the Länder authorities to support their development.

The AHKs (Chambers of Commerce and Industry Abroad) have a threefold role: lobbying on behalf of German companies, providing market access services and bringing foreign and German companies together. They focus on technical assistance, business information, partner search, company coaching, support for trade fair participation, and vocational training. They are the counterpart to the French Chambers of Commerce and Industry Abroad (CCIFE). The AHK network includes over 47,000 companies worldwide.

GTAI (Germany Trade & Invest Agency) provides information on foreign markets through the publication of magazines, market research, seminars and online information services. These services are provided free of charge, unless a company requests otherwise. It does not select the companies to which it sends information. Export promotion for German companies increasingly involves the identification of promising sectors and trends, carried out by an advisory board comprising GTAI members including trade federations. The advisory committee's opinion does not, however, constitute a binding roadmap, as companies remain responsible for their own choices. In terms of supporting companies abroad, the GTAI is positioned in the information product range, thus complementing the activities of the AHKs abroad. It should be noted, however, that a separation of tasks between the various promotional agencies, imposed by Parliament, prevents the GTAI from taking on the promotion of trade fairs and exhibitions. The GTAI also manages iXpos, a website that connects companies with contacts in all the organizations promoting German business abroad.

The German Trade Fair Association (AUMA) also plays an important role in Germany and abroad, as Germany is the world leader in trade fairs for companies. It represents the sector's interests vis-à-vis ministries, parliament and public authorities. It informs exhibitors and visitors about the various activities and offers. In particular, it supports German SMEs in their participation in foreign trade fairs.

Together with the BMWi and the Federal Ministry of Food and Agriculture, it coordinates Germany's activities at trade fairs abroad. The organization of national pavilions at foreign trade fairs (300 per year) is the result of a close partnership between AUMA, the professional organizations (Verbände) and the BMWi. This partnership is an effective tool for promoting German companies abroad. The collective participation of German companies at foreign trade fairs is outsourced to market operators. The organization of two-thirds of German pavilions is entrusted to the major German trade fair companies owned by the cities and Länder, with the remaining third to private companies and consultants. The big fairs are often the organizers of their own shows abroad: over the last twenty years, they have created replicas of their shows all over the world, but especially in emerging countries. Exhibitors naturally follow their lead.

AUMA has a database providing information on almost 5,800 events, trade fairs and exhibitions in Germany and worldwide. There is also a special program for the participation of young innovative companies at national trade fairs. KfW IPEX-Bank, a subsidiary of the KfW Group, Germany's leading public bank, supports German exports by providing financing for the internationalization of companies, exports and development projects. It is involved in a wide range of projects, with a mandate to support German and European exports in the broadest sense. The bank operates on commercial terms, and is required to offer a level of profitability similar to that of the market. In 2020, the bank's new loans amounted to almost 16 billion, out of a total credit volume of 38.1 billion.

State guarantees to support and secure German exports have been managed since 1949 by two private- sector companies, now Euler Hermes (credit insurance) and PwC (investment guarantees), with Euler Hermes as primary insurer. These two private entities are mandated by the BMWi to prepare decisions on the granting of public guarantees. Depending on the size of the guarantee, the decision to grant a guarantee is taken either directly by Euler Hermes, or by the IMA interministerial commission made up of representatives from the various ministries concerned. In 2020, the German government granted a total of almost 16.7 billion guarantees, of which almost 75% were in non-OECD countries. The COVID crisis also led to a 35% increase in applications, mainly for SME products.

To complete this chapter, it is important to return to the definition of several concepts.

The balance of payments is a statistical statement that brings together and arranges in accounting form all the economic and financial transactions of an economy with the rest of the world over a given period. The balance of payments headings, defined by the 6th Balance of Payments Manual (BPM6) in line with the System of National Accounts, are divided between the current account, the capital account and the financial account.

The technology balance of payments is an indicator developed by the OECD to provide a better understanding of the globalization process, through the measurement of international technology transfers between countries. It measures imports and exports of services with a strong technological component: research and development, intellectual property rights and scientific and IT services. These transfers give an indication of a country's ability to sell its technology abroad and to use foreign technologies. They indicate a country's competitive position in the international market for technological knowledge.

The current account includes goods, services, primary income and secondary income. Primary income represents flows that accrue to economic agents for their participation in the production process (compensation of employees), for the provision of financial assets (investment income). Secondary income covers current transfers between residents and non-residents. The capital account includes capital transfers (debt forgiveness, losses on receivables, investment grants and acquisitions and disposals of non-financial non-produced assets). The sum of the current account balance and the capital account corresponds to the nation's financing capacity in the national accounts. The financial account is broken down into direct investments, portfolio investments, derivative financial instruments, other investments and reserve assets. Finally, net errors and omissions is an adjustment item, reflecting statistical discrepancies arising from uncertainties in the coverage rate of certain surveys or differences in method.

From a methodological point of view, and in line with international manuals on the subject (notably the IMF's GPG6), current transactions are based on sources both internal and external to the Bank. For goods, the main source is information provided by customs. However, the balance of goods in the balance of payments covers a wider spectrum. For example, merchanting (the resale of goods that do not cross the French border) is a surplus line that limits the customs goods deficit (balance of 11 billion in 2021).

Two Banks surveys of companies are used to calculate trade in services in France: the follow- up survey of General direct declarants (DDG), for companies with foreign operations in excess of $30 million a year; and the Supplementary survey on international trade in services (ECEIS), which supplements the information obtained from the DDGs. Finally, the travel line is measured by several specific household surveys carried out by the National Banks, supplemented by data on foreign visitors' bankcard spending.

Chapter 6

Business intelligence as a tool for regaining sovereignty.

> In line with the issues of sovereignty and foreign influences shaping the economic, academic and digital environment of advanced economies, it is important to understand the dynamics of state strategies for the organization of business intelligence. After the latest major debates on the subject, after the reorganization of decision-making structures on the issue of economic intelligence in certain countries, and after the implementation of a new public economic security policy by certain governments, it is necessary to make an initial assessment of the actions taken.

This chapter sets out concrete strategies to put economic intelligence back at the heart of public policy, so that governments, local authorities, research establishments, businesses and citizens are better equipped to deal with the economic forces at work in the world today.
Alternatively presented as a dynamic, a culture, a method, a mode of governance, a way of thinking and acting, an approach or even a field of research, economic intelligence aims above all to be on the alert in order to defend the strategic interests of a State, a company, a territory or a research establishment, and to promote its competitiveness. It is based on the following three sets of actions: strategic or competitive intelligence; protection of tangible or intangible assets; and influencing operations.
It has to be said that this is not a recent issue. Several years ago, it was already pointed out that certain developed countries were lagging behind their partners and competitors in terms of business

intelligence. The main causes were the compartmentalization and elitist circulation of information, insufficient links between the public and private sectors, a lack of global interest in business intelligence, and the absence of regular political support. Now, several decades later, it's clear that almost all of the observations made in the past could be repeated. What is needed, therefore, is real awareness and a genuine cultural and organizational change to make business intelligence a common and shared practice at all levels.

Since the 1980s, economically advanced countries have been experiencing a profound, cross-cutting loss of sovereignty, reflected in progressive deindustrialization and a loss of market share for their companies. At the same time, the global economic and geopolitical environment has become increasingly competitive, with foreign powers developing increasingly well-documented offensive practices: capital-intensive threats, attacks on information assets or reputations, capture of knowledge and know-how, cyber-attacks or even adoption of extraterritorial legislation. Against this backdrop, a national strategy drawn up by an interministerial body is becoming increasingly important.

Indeed, in the face of protean threats, there is an urgent need to develop capacities for anticipation, adaptation, analysis and influence, and to define a national business intelligence strategy. This State strategy would be drawn up and implemented by a general economic intelligence authority or agency, attached to the government cabinet, in order to guarantee its multi-disciplinary, inter-ministerial and operational nature. The defensive aspect of this national economic intelligence strategy is in line with the public economic security policy already in place in several countries. While recognizing the improved structuring of these countries in this area, it is important that this defensive aspect be consolidated, particularly with regard to the control of foreign investments and research establishments.

The offensive aspect of such a strategy needs to be developed further, as current actions are essentially defensive in nature. Standards strategy is the main lever to be mobilized, because while several countries are now leaders in terms of standards influence, other powers are catching up fast, with the risk that the voluntary standards applied to their companies will penalize economic competitiveness. So, the main strategies will be : entrusting a general economic intelligence authority or agency, attached to the government cabinet, with the interministerial task of drawing up a national economic intelligence strategy; reinforcing the foreign investment control system by making it compulsory to monitor the commitments made and which have conditioned investment authorization; introduce an annual debate on business intelligence and foreign investment control; provide each research organization with a business intelligence master plan and a business intelligence referent; include in the research tax credit base the costs incurred by small and medium-sized businesses in adapting to standardization.

It is essential to define a national governance structure to implement this strategy. Acknowledging the difficulties economic intelligence has in finding an appropriate position within the State is essential, as for a very long time, several organizational arrangements have been put in place, tried and tested, without the public policy of economic intelligence managing to stabilize or find a lasting organization in several countries. These successive changes of name and administrative form illustrate the concept's difficulty in finding an appropriate and lasting position within the state apparatus. In order to overcome these difficulties, it is essential to create a permanent structure, whose existence would be guaranteed at legislative level, to ensure the continuity of the economic intelligence policy and to encourage more assertive political support. In this respect, the main strategies would be to endow the agency or general authority for economic intelligence with a dedicated multi-disciplinary team, and to appoint a general coordinator who would also be one of the government's cabinet advisors on economic intelligence issues. It is also necessary to appoint ministerial correspondents for economic intelligence and standardization.

In order to better disseminate the business intelligence approach in the regions, we need to involve local authorities to a greater extent. Indeed, to better disseminate economic intelligence, cooperation between the State and local authorities needs to be strengthened, by systematically involving regional councils in the various economic intelligence steering and monitoring committees, and by developing information exchanges and common analysis tools. Under the aegis of the regional prefect, a large number of deconcentrated government departments contribute to the territorial implementation of the current economic security policy: the departmental prefect and his departments, the intelligence services at territorial level, regional administrative departments with economic missions, regional delegates and delegates for strategic information and economic security. The effective circulation of economic information between these players, through the designation of economic intelligence referents, is therefore essential.

In this respect, the creation of a regional economic intelligence committee should be systematized, by introducing a section dedicated to economic intelligence in regional economic development, innovation and internationalization plans. This system should be complemented by a network of business intelligence referents within each deconcentrated State administration in charge of economic or financial missions, and the appointment of a business intelligence referent coordinator in each département. All players should also be trained in business intelligence. While underlining the dynamism of the training on offer, it is felt that it is essential to massively expand this type of training, both within universities and the Top Schools, in both initial and continuing training courses. The aim is not only to train professionals, but also to raise awareness among the general public, so that they are in a state of alert and can commit themselves to economic patriotism. In this way, the growth of a compliance industry will be supported. In favor of greater cooperation between the public and private sectors, it should be noted that the compliance ecosystem - consulting, audit and law firms - in certain countries, should be supported, in particular to face up to the Anglo-Saxon players. Greater mobilization of governments and strategic industry committees is essential.

It would therefore be important to introduce a business intelligence training module into civil service, business and engineering schools, as well as into university courses in research, law and international relations; to support the development of national compliance programs; and to create national reserves in the service of national economic patriotism. A national economic intelligence strategy is essential in an increasingly competitive world shaped by multiple influences. To achieve this, a national economic intelligence strategy (SNIE) must be devised, integrating the defensive and offensive aspects of economic intelligence within a document validated at inter-ministerial level. Entrust the steering of this SNIE to a general economic intelligence agency (SGIE), an interministerial structure reporting directly to the government cabinet. We also need to extend, or even make permanent, the reduction from 25% to 10% of the voting rights threshold triggering control of investments by third-party investors in listed companies. The strategic line should also ensure that the commitments of investors whose investment authorizations are subject to conditions are monitored over time, by entrusting this task to the general directorates of the Treasury in countries that have such directorates.

The introduction of an annual debate on economic intelligence, which will take into account the opinions of the Treasury departments on the control of foreign investments and the fulfillment of investors' commitments, is a priority. This will encourage each research organization to draw up a business intelligence master plan - along the lines of what has been set up in a number of countries - using a common reference framework for research organizations on the risks of capturing scientific and technological information. They should also be encouraged to appoint a business intelligence officer. We also need to define the public standardization strategy and priority subjects within the SNIE. As part of the reform announced in a number of countries, we need to integrate into the tax base the expenses incurred by small and medium-sized businesses in adapting to standardization, and increase the ceiling on the current reimbursement of expenses incurred in participating in standardization meetings. Intelligence services should be tasked with drawing up an annual declassified national report mapping the threats facing their country, along the lines of the ATA report in the United States, which is dedicated to annual threat assessments. This report would include information on economic, technological and scientific threats, as well as on the impact of extraterritorial standards and legislation. We also need to strengthen the ethical framework applicable to the transfer to the private sector of civil servants and contract staff who have held positions in sovereign domains, in intelligence services or in strategic economic intelligence domains as defined by the NIS, by severely restricting their mobility to companies controlled by foreign powers, or even to foreign states themselves.

In terms of decision-making structure, we need to define a national and territorial governance structure for the national business intelligence strategy, to complement the previous provisions. To this end, the national business intelligence strategy should be overseen by a general business intelligence authority or agency, whose long-term survival would be guaranteed by its inclusion in the law. This agency should have the following characteristics: it should have a dedicated multidisciplinary team; it should be headed by a general advisor who is also an advisor to the government cabinet on economic intelligence issues, on the model of the General Secretariat for European Affairs; it would also need a deputy who would be the head of the strategic information and economic security department, to ensure proper coordination with the economic security policy steered by the economic and financial ministries; and it should have relays within each ministry, with ministerial correspondents for economic intelligence and standardization.

It is important to train business intelligence correspondents at district level, so as to increase the number of sensors and empower them to conduct awareness-raising visits, in order to reach small and medium- sized businesses as close as possible to the local area. The system would be optimized by the creation of a network of economic intelligence referents appointed by the departmental authorities, and economic intelligence referents within each decentralized State administration in charge of an economic or financial mission. In order to strengthen State-region cooperation in the service of the SNIE, it is essential to systematize the creation of a regional economic intelligence committee (CRIE) in each region, which would oversee the regional implementation of the public economic intelligence policy (PPIE) and bring together representatives of State services, local authorities, economic operators, research and companies. This CRIE could have two formations: a plenary formation, co-chaired by the regional authorities and the presidents of the regional councils. It would meet at least once a year, and would include all the players involved in economic intelligence; a restricted formation, dedicated to economic security, which would involve the regional council and meet more frequently on operational subjects, in particular threats to local businesses.

The introduction of a business intelligence component in all regional economic development, innovation and internationalization plans (SRDEII) is also called for. This will be complemented by the systematic inclusion of a business intelligence component in new contracts of objectives and performance between governments and chambers of commerce and industry, accompanied by adequate resources to make this a network priority. We also need to enhance the value of business intelligence in certain countries, by introducing a business intelligence training module in all civil service, engineering and business schools, as well as in all university courses in research, social sciences, international relations and law. This will also involve the development of continuing training in business intelligence, and raising awareness among employee and employer unions.

To achieve this, it will be useful to use the knowledge and skills of French business intelligence firms to systematize the search for business intelligence information prior to decision-making, in particular by the Agences des participations de l'État (APE). The approach could also include a business intelligence component in strategic industry committee contracts, and create a biannual conference bringing together all business intelligence players, including local authorities, chambers of commerce and industry, companies and their representatives, trade unions, government departments and academics. We also need to create a national business intelligence research program, with dedicated doctoral research grants. And, to support the development of the French compliance industry (law firms, consulting and audit firms) in the face of Anglo-Saxon players. Finally, the plan will promote the creation of a national reserve to support national economic patriotism.

The first question asked in the course of this appraisal was how to define business intelligence. Despite the apparent simplicity of this question, the answer appears to be different almost every time. Business intelligence is in fact at the crossroads of economic security, economic intelligence and influence. While its interdisciplinary nature makes economic intelligence difficult to grasp, it is this complementary approach that should enable greater effectiveness in defending countries' interests. Business intelligence could thus be defined alternatively as : a collective dynamic aiming for agility through the strategic use of information; a culture of knowledge and anticipation of the international environment; a method based on monitoring, securing and influencing; a mode of governance based on the mastery and exploitation of strategic information to create sustainable value within an entity; a mode of thought and action enabling us to move from a dominant culture and practice of adaptation under constraints to a culture of collective anticipation ; an agile approach aimed at fostering strategic information management in order to identify the risks and opportunities of an ecosystem, with a view to informing the decision-making process; an interdisciplinary field of research combining economics, management sciences, information and communication sciences and technologies, political sciences, law and human sciences, in particular sociology and psychology, and making full use of the potential offered by digital technology; a public policy, the administrative organization of which has not yet been stabilized or completed.

In addition to the various attempts to define business intelligence in terms of its nature, business intelligence is also presented in terms of the objectives and goals it can achieve. For a company, business intelligence is presented above all as a means of reinforcing competitiveness with a view to performance or value creation. For governments, economic intelligence is primarily aimed at defending and promoting their national strategic interests. More broadly, for a state as for a company, economic intelligence has both an offensive and a defensive dimension. This is why the terms "anticipate", "influence" and "protect" are mentioned several times to characterize the actions that can be undertaken in the name of economic intelligence.

Without wishing to enter into an academic and theoretical debate on the definition and translation of the term "economic intelligence", it should be stressed that the definition most often referred to is that which considers economic intelligence to be all coordinated actions of research, processing and distribution, with a view to its exploitation, of information useful to economic players. These various actions are carried out legally, with all the guarantees of protection necessary to preserve the company's assets, under the best conditions of quality, deadlines and cost. This definition lays the foundations for business intelligence. Today, there is no legislative definition of business intelligence, but public authorities have defined it on several occasions since then.

In the interministerial circular on government action in the field of economic intelligence, it is stated that economic intelligence consists of collecting, analyzing, developing, disseminating and protecting strategic economic information, in order to strengthen the competitiveness of a State, a company or a research establishment. For companies, economic intelligence is based on the following three pillars, each of which can give rise to different actions: strategic or competitive intelligence, which consists of researching, gathering and analyzing information in order to make a reliable diagnosis of the company's competitive environment; protection of the company's tangible and intangible assets, to guard against any attempt at plundering and ensure the protection of know-how and strategic information; influence operations, aimed at convincing, seducing or dissuading decision-making bodies operating in the company's direct environment.

Beyond its definition, the relevance of the translation "economic intelligence" is also debated. Business intelligence can be understood as an Anglicism derived from the term "economic intelligence". However, economic intelligence, as commonly understood in non-English-speaking countries, covers the activities of companies and local authorities alike, and is based in part on the processing of open-source information, without recourse to the state privilege of using intelligence techniques. As far as government action is concerned, the concept of economic intelligence could be replaced by the more operational notions of economic security on the defensive side, and economic promotion on the offensive side.

Thus, despite its existence in the public debate for over thirty years, economic intelligence remains a concept that is difficult to translate into action, is unevenly appropriated by different players, and is often widely dispersed. In this respect, certain decrees instituting interministerial delegates for economic intelligence in certain countries, now repealed, provide a good example of the vast scope of actions associated with the notion: the definition of economic intelligence encompassed both objectives without prescribing the means to achieve them - for example, the protection of national economic interests and the scientific, technological and economic assets of states and companies, or the country's influence in international institutions of strategic national interest - as well as more concrete missions - for example, the coordination of a watch, the identification of economic sectors carrying strategic national interests, the implementation of measures to protect sensitive companies and the definition of a standardization strategy.

At national level, economic intelligence is mainly understood in terms of economic security, itself commonly defined as a component of economic intelligence. Economic security would include the defensive aspect of economic intelligence actions, in particular the collection and collation of information aimed at identifying threats and controlling risks, including intangible ones, as well as the implementation of measures to protect companies and other sensitive entities.

For companies, however, these definitions do not allow us to concretely and precisely identify the actions required to put in place a business intelligence approach, over and above technological or competitive intelligence. It has therefore become clear that the perceived vagueness of the notion is unquestionably linked to the cultural and organizational dimension of business intelligence in certain countries. In line with a number of observations made over the past 30 years, it is certain organizational modes and cultural reflexes regarding information sharing that need to be reformed in order to accelerate the development of business intelligence.

Competitive intelligence is part of the broader issue of intangible factors of competitiveness, responding to the need to identify new ways of understanding the balance of power between states and between companies, at a time when the ideological confrontation of the Cold War has given way to globalized, multipolar economic competition. In this context, economic intelligence is seen as a tool for understanding the reorganization of third-country economies, enabling companies and states to understand and anticipate market developments and the strategies of their partner-competitors. Indeed, it is partly thanks to their strategic management of economic information that competitive economies have developed their industries while preserving jobs.

Some countries are still lagging behind in the field of business intelligence, notably the United States, which pioneered business intelligence in the 1950s, Japan, which introduced business intelligence systems in the 1970s, and Germany and Sweden. A comparative analysis of the various business intelligence systems highlights the fact that they are closely linked to the history and culture of each country. However, the few business intelligence practices observed in countries just starting out in 1994 - rarely going beyond strategic intelligence - were imported from abroad, stripped of their cultural foundation, without being associated with a global understanding of the issues at stake and the dissemination of a business intelligence culture. As a result, in 1994, business intelligence in some countries was rare, and even non-existent outside the general management of a few large companies in strategic sectors such as energy, automobiles and telecommunications.

The main obstacles to the spread of business intelligence are cultural and historical in origin: the compartmentalization of companies and administrations alike, and the lack of a culture of consultation, make it very difficult to disseminate effective business intelligence systems. One of our main conclusions is that business intelligence is inextricably linked to the notion of networks. The network itself was set up in consultation with local authorities, consular bodies, government departments, industries, trade unions and service companies.

Here are the main weaknesses of the tool: an elitist circulation of information, which largely escapes the industrial fabric of small and medium-sized enterprises (SMEs), which are nonetheless indispensable to economic life; a culture of economic intelligence intimately linked to the trade, with no concerted collective practice disseminated throughout an entire company or administration; a poorly mastered culture of secrecy based on a conception of information as a source of power, leading to excessively rigid administrative practices in terms of confidentiality, hindering the fine, mastered selection of open information ; cultural and organizational blockages, with relations between the public and private sectors still tinged with mistrust, and converging interests rarely recognized; an overall lack of interest in analyzing and gaining in-depth knowledge of the different cultures a company may encounter in its market, to the detriment of adapting methods and organizational modes. A pronounced belief in the universal nature of cultural values handicaps the ability to adapt to the new competitive realities of globalized markets in many countries. Several countries have lost competitiveness and are becoming deindustrialized, international competition between companies is extremely fierce, and geo-economic relations between states resemble economic warfare.

Our ambition here, however, is to adopt a more operational approach. Despite undeniable progress in terms of awareness and information, the political impetus needed to truly disseminate a culture of economic intelligence has never been forthcoming.

The shortcomings identified earlier in these countries are still considered valid: institutional and cultural blockages, particularly in terms of compartmentalization and verticality; university mistrust of business; the relative weakness of intelligence services compared to their Anglo-Saxon equivalents; timid structuring of the standardization and compliance sector. It was therefore necessary to formulate a number of concrete proposals for implementing a genuine public policy on business intelligence.

In the absence of a long-term business intelligence strategy in these countries, and despite our best efforts, we have to admit that most of the recommendations made in the past could still be repeated. We need to be more prescriptive about the resources that the State can mobilize to support an operational business intelligence strategy, in both its offensive and defensive aspects. It has to be said, however, that the current context calls for a major leap forward in the field of economic intelligence, a pillar in the reconquest of economic sovereignty. Numerous recent examples attest to the inadequacy of business intelligence.

Since the 1980s, there has been a gradual loss of sovereignty that is far more far-reaching and far more profound than has hitherto been the case (economic dependencies and fragilities having been accentuated by the crises of the last three years). Above all, these dependencies and fragilities have been reinforced by the naïveté, or worse, inaction, of public authorities.

In a way, economic intelligence is an extension of economic sovereignty. Lack of anticipation, lack of vigilance, lack of analysis of competitive developments in markets of strategic importance to industry, or even underestimation of the economic intelligence strategies of other countries, has meant that the economy has suffered on many occasions from a lack of culture and political strategy in this area.

It is important to emphasize the need for every country to adopt a long-term, more aggressive business intelligence strategy. Without claiming to be an exhaustive list, it is advisable to recall the following situations, while putting them in perspective of the lack of strategic culture within political, administrative and economic leaders:

- the failure of the Mirage 2000-5 sale to Finland in 1992, an initial analysis of which should have been published in the Martre report in 1994;
- the loss of strategic information during the failed merger between Renault and Volvo between 1992 and 1993;
- the underestimation of the scale of the call for a boycott of French products following the announcement of the resumption of nuclear testing in the Pacific in 1995;
- the sale of Péchiney, the packaging and aluminum champion, to Canada's Alcan in 2003;
- the failure of the Rafale sale to Morocco in 2007, which could be explained by the lack of coordination between the Armament Procurement Agency and Dassault, as well as by the United States' strategy of combining economic and diplomatic support for issues of regional interest;
- the case of a former Michelin executive who offered to sell strategic information to its competitor Bridgestone in 2007;
- the failure to sell Rafales to Brazil in 2009, which could be explained by Sweden's strategy of weaving support networks for local businesses at provincial level through cooperation and innovation support contracts;
- the failure to win the contract to build a high-speed train in Saudi Arabia in 2010 because SNCF and Alstom failed to take account of the country's specific cultural characteristics;
- the Gemplus affair, a French smart card company that was spied on by US intelligence services;

- the takeover of the French company Arcelor by the Indian group Mittal Steel in 2006 and the risk of losing industrial know-how;
- the sale of Alstom's nuclear submarine turbines to the American company General Electric in 2015;
- the sale of Alcatel-Lucent, the flagship of telecommunications equipment and submarine cable manufacturing through its subsidiary Alcatel Submarine Networks, to the Finnish group Nokia in 2015-2016;
- the sale of Technip, a leader in oilfield engineering, to Texas-based FMC Technologies in 2017;
- the planned sale of Atlantic Shipyards to Italy's Fincantieri, in association with a Chinese state-owned conglomerate aiming to become the world leader in the cruise ship market by 2020.

By mentioning these few examples, we aim to highlight the lack of a business intelligence culture and awareness of the economic power relations at work, even today. A better business intelligence culture and greater sharing of information would enable us to contribute more effectively to the fight against deindustrialization, the loss of industrial know-how and economic competitiveness. Although progress has been made in recent years, and a growing body of work, particularly in parliament, is contributing to greater awareness of these issues in public debate, recent cases demonstrate the need to step up efforts in the fields of economic intelligence, monitoring and influence, in order to better anticipate the response of public authorities when such a response is required. For example, in the case of the cancellation of the submarine sale contract between Naval Group and Australia, weak signals were not perceived, no doubt due to a lack of ongoing strategic and information intelligence activities in this part of the world. Once again, recent events demonstrate how business intelligence is an essential tool for anticipating risks.

While there is still progress to be made in spreading the culture of economic intelligence more widely and adopting more offensive practices in this area, we welcome the structuring, over the last few years, of a genuine public economic security policy (PPSE) at State level, with new governance and a new territorial approach. Countries lagging behind, however, should be called upon to adopt a genuine public economic intelligence policy, whose scope is broader than economic security alone - which excludes, in particular, intelligence and influence activities - and to strengthen its offensive component. Recent efforts to structure the State are part of a gradual awareness and change of posture on the part of certain countries, which are becoming increasingly offensive, both in the discourse of their leaders and in the measures adopted. Here are just a few examples of the measures implemented in recent years at European and national level, which are helping to regain economic and industrial sovereignty, and to increase alertness:

- updating the European regulation protecting against the effects of the extraterritorial application of legislation adopted by a third country, as well as actions based on or resulting from it;
- the adoption of a European regulation establishing a framework for the screening of foreign direct investment in the European Union;
- the gradual tightening of national controls on foreign investment in France, particularly in light of the pandemic and the war in Ukraine;
- the adoption by the European Commission of a 5G toolkit to enable us to act together in the face of threats to our strategic autonomy posed by certain telecoms equipment manufacturers;
- setting up the European Innovation Council and the European Defence Fund;
- accelerating major projects of common European interest (PIIEC) in strategic industrial and economic sectors;
- the adoption of an endowed Chips Act to build a European semiconductor industry;
- speeding up the work of the European Parliament and national parliaments on foreign influence and interference;

- the adoption of a legislative arsenal enabling us to better combat our digital vulnerabilities, in particular with the adoption of European regulations on digital services (RSN), digital markets (RMN) and data governance (RGA).

In order to consider the development of business intelligence, it is essential to be aware of the economic and geopolitical context in which the State and companies operate. We should bear in mind the fierce competition between member states within the European Union, as well as the strong Sino-American rivalry, the consequences of which are felt as far afield as Europe. Without denying the benefits of an open economy, this observation should lead to greater protection for companies and their interests in the face of foreign influences, or even interference, hostile takeover attempts, technological or intellectual property capture, informational capture, or even reputational threats.

From this point of view, the risks threatening the economy and businesses are very real and are tending to increase - also because these risks are increasingly well documented. For example, according to the Strategic Information and Economic Security Service (SISSE) of the Directorate General for Enterprise (DGE), several economic security alerts were recorded and processed in 2022, representing a 45% increase on 2021, and more than double on 2020. While the precise nature of these alerts and the companies and entities they concern are classified, it has been indicated that these alerts are of two main types: a potential takeover by foreign economic players, which is characteristic of a capital- intensive threat; and attempts to capture intellectual property and strategic information, which is characteristic of attacks on companies' information assets.

According to the French Treasury, the threat of capital investment remains particularly strong today. In 2022, for example, a number of applications were filed under foreign investment control regulations, and a large number of investment operations were authorized by the Minister, 54% of which were accompanied by conditions of commitment for investors. Over 58% of these investments were made by non-European end investors - i.e. from outside the EU or the European Economic Area (EEA) - mainly from the UK, the USA and Canada. Within the EU and EEA, over 40% of investments came from end investors in Germany, Luxembourg and Ireland.

In addition to these indicators, we must also bear in mind the importance and increase in extra-territorial legislation to which companies are subject. A complete economic assessment of extraterritorial measures is therefore called for, in order to better quantify the scale of the costs incurred by companies' failure to protect themselves, as this work does not currently exist. Since 2008, it is estimated that European companies have paid out nearly $8 billion under the US Foreign Corrupt Practices Act (FCPA) alone. Outside the framework of the FCPA alone, the amounts are even higher, with ExpertActions Group estimating this figure at over 20 billion dollars - a figure that is set to rise further with the tightening of extra-territorial sanctions. Monitoring the extraterritorial legal frameworks of other countries is therefore an essential part of business intelligence.

Chapter 7

Design national business intelligence strategies with resources to match ambitions

> In order not to remain a dead letter, the implementation of a national economic intelligence strategy (SNIE) should respect the resolutely multidisciplinary nature of economic intelligence. It must therefore be defined in consultation with all the administrations concerned - and not just the economic and financial ministries - and formalized in a document validated at interministerial level. It must also be overseen by an interministerial structure, so as to go beyond the economic or security aspects of business intelligence and embrace all its aspects (research, higher education, control of normative, social, industrial and ecological risks, etc.).

In addition to economic security, the defensive aspect of economic intelligence, this economic intelligence strategy should include a more offensive aspect, giving administrations, local authorities and businesses the capacity to anticipate and adapt to changes in the economic landscape, with a view to preserving and strengthening our competitiveness. We therefore need to devise a national business intelligence strategy (SNIE) integrating the defensive and offensive aspects of business intelligence within a document validated at inter-ministerial level. Entrust the steering of this SNIE to an interministerial authority, the SGIE (general authority for business intelligence).
The Public Policy for Economic Security (PPSE) embodies what should be the defensive aspect of a national economic intelligence

strategy. The PPSE aims to ensure the defense and promotion of the country's economic, industrial and scientific interests, including the tangible and intangible assets that are strategic to the economy. It therefore includes defending French companies and research organizations against foreign interference. Many countries have adopted a foreign investment control policy based on a balance between the principle of free relations between these countries and foreigners and the defense of national interests. Thus, by decree issued on the report of the minister responsible for the economy, governments can make any movement of capital between states and foreign countries subject to declaration, prior authorization or control.

Certain foreign investments are subject to prior authorization by the Minister of the Economy: investments in activities that are involved, even on an occasional basis, in the exercise of public authority, or are likely to undermine public order, public security or national defense interests, or involve the research, production or marketing of arms and explosives. Authorization may be subject to conditions designed to ensure that the planned investment will not undermine national interests - for example, conditions relating to the maintenance and continuity of sensitive activities, the preservation of the target entity's knowledge and know-how, governance or the communication of information to governments.

The precise list of activities covered by foreign investment control, which falls within the scope of regulations, has been progressively extended: a list of fields in which investments are subject to prior authorization, ranging from gambling to cryptology and private security activities; this list has been extended to include activities involving equipment, goods or services essential to guaranteeing the supply of electricity, water or energy, the protection of public health, and the security and integrity of transport networks and electronic communications services; this list also includes activities involving the processing, transmission or storage of data, the compromise or disclosure of which is likely to undermine the exercise of other activities on the list, as well as activities involving infrastructures, goods or services essential to guaranteeing food safety, or the publication of political and general information in the press.

In addition to the activities concerned, the threshold for holding voting rights or capital triggering a foreign investment control procedure, set at 33.33% since 2005, has recently been lowered: a decree has lowered the threshold triggering a takeover, and therefore a possible prior authorization procedure, to 25% when the investment is made by investors of another nationality; the threshold of 25% of voting rights triggering a control procedure for investments made in listed companies has been lowered to 10%. This temporary measure, which was due to apply, has been extended and should be made permanent. Lastly, the Minister for the Economy has been given enhanced prerogatives to ensure effective control of these investments. The Act strengthens the Minister's control powers by enabling him to issue an injunction to the foreign investor, possibly accompanied by a fine, when an investment has been made without prior authorization. Where the conditions attached to the authorization have been disregarded, it can also take measures ranging from injunctions to withdrawal of the investment authorization.

In cases where national interests are likely to be compromised, the Minister is authorized to take one or more precautionary measures, such as the withdrawal of irregularly acquired voting rights. Lastly, the Ministry of the Economy may take into account a possible link with a foreign government or public body to justify a refusal. On the other hand, parliamentary control and information on foreign investment control activities have been strengthened: governments publish annual statistics on foreign investment in their country, and submit an annual report on government action to control foreign investment. On the other hand, it seems necessary to strengthen the monitoring of investors' commitments.

Despite this recent strengthening of the system, companies remain vulnerable to the predatory strategies of foreign powers. In legal terms, the framework for E.I. control gives the Minister of the Economy powers to protect national interests. In practice, however: because IE control is not part of an overall economic intelligence strategy, the relevant government departments are generally faced with the fait accompli of an investment decision by a third party in the region, whereas a strategy of monitoring, sharing and processing strategic economic information might have enabled the departments to anticipate the takeover; authorization refusals are very rare: they must be justified by the investor's good repute, or by the fact that attaching conditions to the Minister's authorization would not be sufficient to ensure the preservation of public safety, public order or the interests of national defense. In 2022, foreign investment transactions eligible for IE control were authorized. Of these, 53% were subject to conditions designed to protect national interests.

In practice, therefore, the effective protection of national interests in the context of IE control is conditional on the proper definition of conditions capable of providing guarantees to French companies, and on investors' subsequent compliance with these conditions. However, authorizations may be subject to conditions that are insufficient for the strategic importance of the company for each country. In this respect, the example of the planned takeover of Chantiers de l'Atlantique by Italy's Ficantieri is edifying, even if it was finally abandoned in early 2021 after much procrastination. The agreement reached in 2018 between the French company STX and its main Italian competitor, Ficantieri, provided for Ficantieri to obtain 50% of the capital, to which would be added 1% in the form of a long-term loan from the Agence des participations de l'État. This loan transferred operational control of the company to Ficantieri, but was revocable at certain times if the Italian group failed to meet its industrial commitments, which included not cutting jobs for five years, maintaining the existing order book in France and not transferring technology outside Europe. After twelve years, the loan was to be terminated and the 1% sold to Fincantieri.

The Economic Affairs Committee criticized the flawed content of the 2018 compromise. In particular, it did not allow the State to intervene in the event of serious and imminent threats to the integrity of Atlantic ShipyardsAtlantic Shipyards, nor did it provide for any penalties for Ficantieri in the event of non- compliance with its contractual commitments. Similarly, the takeover of part of Alstom's activities by General Electric (GE) in 2015 showed that time-limited commitments are often ignored as soon as they expire. In 2019, for example, GE paid $50 million into a reindustrialization fund after failing to meet its commitment to create a thousand jobs in France. The experience of the merger between Technip and Texas-based FMC Technologies in 2017 showed that the announcement of a marriage between equals, with equal governance, can then result in an absorption, with the blessing of a 5% state shareholding in the company via the investment bank. Indeed, despite announcements of parity in governance, two years later only three members of Technip FMC's executive committee were former Technip employees. The legal reinforcement of foreign investment control begun several years ago must therefore be pursued and integrated into an overall economic intelligence strategy. The lowering of the threshold for capital ownership or voting rights triggering E.I. control implemented during the health crisis is a welcome measure, which is not unprecedented: Spain adopted a temporary measure lowering the control threshold for non-EU investments to 10% at the start of the health crisis, and recently extended it to 2024; Germany also has a control threshold of 10% of voting rights for foreign investments in certain sensitive sectors such as military technology.

Beyond the thresholds for controlling EIs, monitoring and evaluation of the implementation of conditions attached to investment authorizations must be stepped up. Conditions may be set for a long period of time - for example, more than ten years - and it is important that they are complied with for the entire duration, otherwise the validity of the investment authorization may be called into question. It is therefore crucial that central government departments have sufficient resources to monitor compliance with these conditions over time, and to ascertain, on the basis of documents and on site if necessary, that commitments have actually been implemented: an investor's declaration of intent is no proof of compliance with the conditions attached to the authorization. The control exercised by the services of the Minister of the Economy must be commensurate with the extensive prerogatives he has to enforce these conditions. What's more, the evaluation of these commitments is left entirely in the hands of the central administration, with no consultation, association or information of either the local authorities or the national representatives. While the publications and government reports to parliamentary assemblies introduced by the law are welcome, a specific time for annual debate dedicated to the control of EIs would enable national representation to address its questions to the government and relay the concerns of local authorities regarding foreign investments made on their territory.

It is also important to better protect the world of research from foreign influences. Surveys of state influence in the academic world reveal that the risks of foreign interference in academia are widely underestimated. It would be advisable to reaffirm the need to strengthen economic intelligence resources. In reality, most developed countries are prime targets. Their academic and research establishments are fragile: salaries and working conditions are less favorable than in other countries. These establishments are subject to contradictory injunctions to welcome foreign students and tighten controls, while at the same time being autonomous in their administrative management. Finally, the research community's culture of openness makes it reluctant to adopt a proactive attitude to detecting attempts at interference and defending national scientific interests. To reinforce the academic world's alertness to foreign influences, it is recommended, for example, to create an observatory of foreign influences and their impact on higher education and research, which would bring together academics and government departments in an inter-ministerial approach. It is also important to raise awareness of these issues among local authorities, particularly regions and major cities, given their role on the boards of higher education establishments.

On a national level, we recommend making transparency and reciprocity the cardinal principles of all international university cooperation, and extending the system for protecting the scientific and technical heritage of nations to all university disciplines, adapting it to the specific challenges of the humanities and social sciences, which are excluded. Indeed, sensitive research activities are among the strategic assets to be protected. In the current context of tensions over energy resources, critical materials and global supply chains, the race for critical technologies is exacerbated: given their often dual nature, they often generate both a competitive and a strategic advantage.

Threats to the research community can take many forms: recruitment of staff seeking to capture knowledge rather than advance the scientific community; candidates with a brilliant track record whose performance on the job casts doubt on their identity, or whose level appears to be far higher than that required for the position; unbalanced collaborations; detour of the initial purpose of research to offensive ends; paid interviews with in-house experts under the guise of market research; presence on the premises at abnormal hours; filming in nearby laboratories, and so on.

To this end, practical guides and vademecums along the lines of those drawn up by the Interministerial Delegation for Economic Intelligence on guidelines for the international mobility of scientists and experts should be widely distributed by the relevant public administrations to the organizations they oversee. Each month, the General Directorates of Internal Security publish a "Flash ingérence" (interference flash), which presents the economic interference actions of which local companies are regularly victims. Some editions may be dedicated to the risks associated with capturing know-how in fundamental research. In these editions, the General Directorates of Internal Security highlight the fact that the risks of interference in basic research are much underestimated in comparison with applied research. Yet fundamental research is largely targeted by foreign universities seeking to make up for scientific or technological backwardness. These foreign states can then use the results of this basic research for applied purposes, to develop products on their own: there is therefore a considerable risk that this research will be used for military purposes, creating a major reputational risk for local research structures.

To curb these risks, the General Directorates for Internal Security recommend that research organizations make all their staff aware of the need to protect the scientific and technical heritage of nations, ensure that buildings are sufficiently secure, and consider the risks of any research carried out being diverted for military purposes. The creation of restricted zones, with defined administrative protection, may also be envisaged for part of the laboratory, in order to exclude certain risky profiles. The master plan for economic intelligence of the General Commissariats for Atomic Energy and Alternative Energies (CEA) has a master plan for economic intelligence (SDIE) drawn up under the supervision of a steering committee comprising representatives of the general management. The SDIE is divided into two parts: a strategic section to define the main orientations of the business intelligence mission in the short and medium term, and an operational section to define the action plan for its implementation, notably concerning business skills, technical tools and financial requirements in terms of investment and operation.

The implementation of the SDIE is based on a network-based organization of the economic intelligence function within the CEA: placing the CEA in a good position, the SDIE specifies that, as a cross-functional function by nature, economic intelligence must participate in the selective decompartmentalization of information through a network-based organization, based on light structures in terms of resources, distributed within the various operational and functional departments. The network's leadership is entrusted to a referent positioned within a cross-functional department, to go beyond the purely security-related dimension of the discipline. The structuring of this business intelligence approach was included in the contract of objectives and performance (COP) signed between the French government and the CEA.

Public authorities must therefore encourage the development of business intelligence initiatives within research organizations. The Ministry of Higher Education and Research concludes contracts of objectives and performance (COP) or means (COM) with the public higher education and research establishments under its supervision. These COP contracts are an effective way of encouraging the implementation of business intelligence practices. What's more, they represent a means of reaching a large part of the research community, through public research organizations and the hundreds of universities, prestigious schools and other higher education establishments, such as university innovation clusters (PUI). We therefore need to encourage each research organization to draw up a business intelligence master plan - along the lines of the one set up within the CEA - using a common reference framework for research organizations on the risks of capturing scientific and technological information. They should also be encouraged to appoint a business intelligence officer.

A state's ability to influence international economic standards, i.e. the rules of the game in a globalized economy, is an essential element of competitiveness for companies. As such, normative influence is a component of economic intelligence, or even soft power, which remains underestimated in many countries. These voluntary standards are omnipresent in our daily lives: they are used to determine the design of electrical outlets, the dimensions of sheets of paper or the water content of honey. Drawn up within a technical framework by a network of private organizations at national and international level, they are applied voluntarily by economic players - who have every interest in following them, not least because they condition access to markets.

These standards are never innocent: they set modes of governance, give players the means to anticipate or curb competition, and determine strategies for the production and exchange of goods and services, and so on. They are therefore an issue of competitiveness and sovereignty, especially for sectors undergoing growth and change. It is becoming increasingly difficult to separate technology from politics. Failing to anticipate changes in standards, or even being the author of such changes, may result in missing out on a competitive advantage, or even being subjected to changes in regulations, as voluntary standards increasingly support and equip the implementation of regulations. It is not uncommon for regional institutions to ask the three regional standards organizations to draw up standards contributing to the proper implementation of the law, by means of reference systems or methodologies.

States and, indirectly, companies therefore have every interest in developing a strategy of normative influence: whoever masters the norm masters the market. However, the majority of countries have adopted a relatively "wait-and-see" attitude: they remain well placed in international rankings, but their strategy of presence and influence is insufficient, in a context where the development of standards is subject to the same competition as products: 90% of current standards are developed at international level. States, via their national standards bodies, therefore compete fiercely to hold committee secretariats and formulate proposals within working groups.

Already in 2008, ExpertActions Group on international expertise deplored the fact that some countries, such as France, have little influence on the development of standards and soft law, and struggle to mobilize experts on missions for international organizations or other states. In 2013, the Chair of Institutional Governance & Strategic Leadership Research underlined the insufficient ambition of these countries' normative influence strategy and the fragility of their positions. The barometer established since then by the Association de normalisation shows that, in 2022, France can boast a favorable position in terms of standards influence, measured by the number of committees for which it provides secretariat services: this country ranks fairly well internationally for its presence on committees of the International Organization for Standardization (ISO) and the International Electrotechnical Commission (IEC). However, it is far outstripped by Germany and the United States, and is neck-and-neck with Japan, the United Kingdom and China by one secretariat.

This country's favorable position is therefore fragile. They are threatened by the rapid rise of China, which was responsible for the secretariats of just 30 committees in 2010, compared with around 80 in 2022, while the influence of the countries in question is stagnating or even shrinking. This Chinese push is part of an offensive strategy to place Chinese nationals at the head of specialized international organizations, such as the International Telecommunication Union (ITU), where China was Director General from 2015 to 2022, and the United Nations Industrial Development Organization (UNIDO) from 2013 to 2021, the International Civil Aviation Organization (ICAO), where she was Secretary General from 2015 to 2021, and the Food and Agriculture Organization of the United Nations (FAO), where the Director General, who has been Chinese since 2019, was re-elected for 4 years in July 2023.

Germany enjoys a stable and advanced position in Europe. On the energy front, its strategy of normative influence is far more aggressive than that of France: in May 2021, the School of Economic Warfare already demonstrated how the German strategy of promoting renewable energies and gas to the detriment of nuclear power at European level was based on an organized network of political parties, control of strategic positions and close links between interest representatives and German administrations. In June 2023, a new alert report by the School of Economic Warfare denounced the interference of German political foundations, some of which are backed to the tune of over 90% by the German state and public authorities, in the French public sphere, with a view to reducing the credibility of the nuclear industry.

Back in 2013, the Chair of Institutional Governance & Strategic Leadership Research called for international regulatory and standards issues to be decompartmentalized and integrated into a dynamic economic intelligence approach in order to link public policy and standardization. Similarly, in 2017, ExpertActions Group highlighted the lack of a collective standards strategy among industries, and the absence of consultation between the State, local authorities, businesses and standards bodies. Since then, a number of commendable initiatives have been implemented. For example, the major challenge - Securing, making reliable and certifying systems based on artificial intelligence - launched by the General Investment Authority includes a major standards component, which has led to the development of a national strategic roadmap for artificial intelligence standardization, intended to be taken to European level and to structure the concerted participation of players in the work carried out by CEN and CENELEC to equip the future regulation on artificial intelligence.

A standardization component should therefore be systematically included in sectoral public policies implemented by the French government, in order to promote a coordinated and effective approach in international standardization forums. These sectoral standardization components should be grouped together in a standardization section of the national economic intelligence strategy (SNIE), identifying subjects of strategic importance over a multi-year period. To encourage companies to get involved in standardization bodies, a commitment which can consume time and resources given the technical nature of the subjects, the coverage of standardization expenses via the research tax credit (CIR) could be reinforced. Today, the CIR takes into account half of the standardization expenses relating to the company's products, defined as follows: salaries and social security charges relating to the periods during which employees take part in official standardization meetings; other expenses relating to these same operations, set at a flat rate of 30% of these salaries; the costs of participation in official standardization meetings by heads of sole proprietorships and managers of legal entities, up to a limit of $437.35 per day. At present, expenses are excluded if they do not take part in the upstream definition of standards, but instead adapt products to standards that have already been defined. In order to support SMEs wishing to conquer new markets, and to avoid penalizing them for the inadequacy of their standards influence strategy, it would therefore make sense to include these expenses, for VSEs and SMEs only, in the CIR as part of the reform of the latter. The ability of any organization to capture, process and share information is the key to a successful business intelligence strategy, and more specifically to its offensive aspect, which is currently lacking. ExpertActions Group has identified three organizational and cultural obstacles to effective economic information management: a cultural change is therefore necessary, in both companies and government departments, in favor of a more open, horizontal vision, more conducive to consultation, questioning and adaptation. In this respect, the unified economic security reference framework drawn up by the Strategic Information and Economic Security Department should be disseminated and adopted by all government departments responsible for implementing any aspect of the PPSE. This unified reference framework is cross-functional: it includes a confidential national list of strategic companies to be protected as a priority, a list of critical technologies and a list of laboratories and public research organizations to be protected as a priority.

For example, the Treasury Department in some countries has identified the vulnerability of metal product supplies in 2021, using three criteria: the share of non-European imports, the concentration of imports on a small number of non-EU suppliers, and the inadequacy of European production. Earlier work, such as a Tresor-eco note, assessed supply vulnerability using two different criteria. Not only should the results of this work be shared and used by other administrations, but the methodologies used to identify vulnerable supplies should be unified within a reference framework, in order to provide a clear strategy. In this respect, some experts on economic sovereignty have already called for a comprehensive mapping of the economy's vulnerabilities.

What's more, best practices in information sharing thanks to artificial intelligence need to be disseminated within the administrations concerned and within companies: the collective capacity to process information cannot suffer any conservatism. Artificial intelligence can be put to good use in the service of business intelligence, since the latter is based on the intelligent collection, processing and dissemination of business information, which is often accessible in open source format. To encourage cultural change and the spread of a business intelligence culture, information sharing must involve all government departments, including the most secretive: ExpertActions Group mentioned the structuring role played by intelligence services in the United States, which were already playing a quasi-advisory role with government departments and even companies. In fact, the declassified annual threats assessment (ATA) published by the CIA has become a structuring report, eagerly awaited each year by American and international business players alike. Basically, intelligence services should be tasked with drawing up a declassified annual national report mapping the threats weighing on countries, along the lines of the ATA report in the United States, which is dedicated to annual threat assessments.

Although any business intelligence approach is inseparable from the notion of networking, this does not mean that information should be accessible to all: business intelligence aims to reduce the distribution of information in silos and promote cross-functionality, while protecting strategic information. In this respect, ExpertActions Group noted that, according to the people interviewed, the number of people entitled to defence secrecy was excessive, while certain sensitive functions directly affecting economic and financial security were nevertheless exempt from secrecy. It therefore proposed a rethink of the number and quality of personnel with defence secrecy clearance within government departments, so that the relevant departments within the intelligence services could carry out their investigative work under the best possible conditions.

The study also identified the risk to national security posed by private intelligence and security companies, which are often disguised under other names such as business intelligence consultancy, lobbying, communications, etc. It also pointed out that the very nature of their business calls for special precautions. However, he pointed out that the very nature of their business requires special precautions; their activity is not neutral with regard to respect for public freedoms; and companies need trusted partners offering guarantees of ethics, confidentiality and professionalism. It therefore proposed the creation of an ethics committee for these companies, tasked with examining the development and implementation of an ethics label, as well as the creation of a register of these companies. Today, the supervision of these companies is still an issue, to which must be added that of possible mobility between the public and private sectors in the field of intelligence and security. The Group points out that this issue was raised on numerous occasions during our hearings, noting that many former military or intelligence personnel are now working for international business intelligence firms or foreign companies.

We also need to strengthen the ethical framework applicable to the transfer to the private sector of civil servants and contract employees who have held positions in sovereign domains, in intelligence services or in strategic business intelligence domains as defined by the national business intelligence strategy, by severely restricting their mobility to companies controlled by foreign powers, or even to foreign states themselves. As a result of these studies, it was felt that the State should play a more stimulating role in economic intelligence, in order to initiate a more collective and shared management of information between administrations, local authorities and the private sector. To this end, a national inter-ministerial coordination body was set up at State level: the Committee for Competitiveness and Economic Security (CCSE). The CCSE was made up of seven personalities, appointed for a period of three years and chosen for their experience, authority or competence, in order to inform the Government's choices on issues of competitiveness and economic security.

The secretariat of the CCSE was provided by the General Secretariat of National Defense (SGDN), which even then reflected a rather defensive approach to economic intelligence in a context of accelerating globalization and a feeling, already, of a gradual loss of economic sovereignty and competitiveness. The aim was for companies to take more effective account of the threats and opportunities emerging on international markets, and to gain a better understanding of the many global factors that today condition scientific, industrial and economic development on an international scale. Although the CCSE has set up an interministerial working group for policy, defense and economic intelligence, which has delivered its initial conclusions, this organization has not lasted long enough for a satisfactory assessment to be made. The Agency for the Diffusion of Technological Information (ADIT) has indicated, however, that the

CCSE was a coordinating body that functioned relatively well, notably because it brought together the major directors of central administration.

In some cases, a change of government and the end of the committee members' terms of office have interrupted the CCSE process, and inter-ministerial work is now carried out by the senior defense and security official at the Ministry of the Economy, Finance and Industry. In some cases, a senior economic intelligence officer has been placed under the SGDN. At the same time, in some cases, an economic intelligence coordination service (SCIE) has been set up, attached to the General Secretariat of the Economic and Financial Ministries (MEF). In parallel to the existence of the SCIE, an interministerial delegation for economic intelligence was set up, with three successive interministerial delegates: interministerial delegate for economic intelligence, reporting to the Secretary General of the Ministry for the Economy; interministerial delegate for economic intelligence, reporting to the Head of Government; interministerial delegate for economic intelligence.

A turning point in the administrative organization of business intelligence has been reached, insofar as a genuine interministerial structure has been set up, after several years of steering by either the SGDN or the MEFs. According to the decree on the interministerial delegate for economic intelligence, the delegate reports directly to the Prime Minister, works in direct liaison with the ministries concerned and the SGDN, and is responsible for the following main tasks: drawing up public policy on economic intelligence; chairing the interministerial steering committee; coordinating a network of regional correspondents and diplomatic correspondents; informing the authorities about economic, scientific, industrial and commercial developments; identifying risks and threats likely to affect strategic organizations and companies; organizing training, communication and awareness-raising campaigns on economic intelligence.

However, the difficulties encountered by this interministerial delegation in implementing a genuine business intelligence policy and reporting directly to the head of government were highlighted,

as it certainly suffered from a lack of strong political impetus on the subject. Hesitations between the need for an interministerial steering body embracing the multi-disciplinary nature of economic intelligence, and the need for a steering body run by the MEFs, persisted until a new structure dedicated to economic security was set up. Given the difficulties of coordination and the persistent hesitations linked to the positioning of economic intelligence within the State apparatus, it was decided to merge certain structures in order to create a Strategic Information and Economic Security Commission (CISSE) and a department dedicated to strategic information and economic security (SISSE). Today, the Director General for Enterprises is also the Commissioner for Strategic Information and Economic
Security, while the SISSE is also attached to the Directorate General for Enterprises (DGE) within the MEF.

The decree defines the missions of CISSE, whose main task is to draw up, in conjunction with the relevant ministries and the General Secretariat for National Defense and Security (SGDSN), public policy on the protection and promotion of economic, industrial and scientific interests. CISSE's mission, which is still in force today, is to contribute to the development of public policies relating to: the protection and promotion of the economy's tangible and intangible assets; compliance standards applicable to companies in terms of financial relations with foreign countries, the fight against corporate fraud and corruption, and social and environmental responsibility; the defense of digital sovereignty; and standardization strategies.

In support of CISSE, SISSE carries out the following missions, with a view to protecting France's strategic assets from foreign threats: to identify sectors, technologies and companies of economic, industrial and scientific interest, and to centralize strategic information concerning them; to contribute to the development of the Government's position on foreign investment; to inform State authorities of persons, companies and organizations presenting an interest or representing a threat; to ensure the application of the provisions of the law relating to the communication of documents and information of an economic, commercial, industrial, financial or technical nature to foreign natural persons or legal entities. In addition to its national activities, SISSE has set up a territorial network of delegates attached to the regional directorates for the economy, employment, labor and solidarity (Dreets), which report to the regional prefects. There is a shared feeling of satisfaction with the actions carried out by SISSE today. However, it should be noted that the entry into force of the decree and the creation of the SISSE mark the decline in the use of the term economic intelligence, reflecting the desire to implement a new public policy now essentially focused on economic security.

We must emphasize the efforts made by the State and its administration to structure economic security, with the implementation of a new governance structure and several bodies for consultation, dialogue and exchange, which have met with the satisfaction of the players interviewed. Firstly, at central government level, a liaison committee for economic security (COLISE) has been set up. Chaired by the General Authority for National Defense and Security (SGDSN), with CISSE acting as COLISE secretariat, this committee is tasked with preparing the instruction of decisions by the National Defense and Security Council (CDSN), in the field of economic security. The committee also plays an important role in interministerial coordination between the relevant ministries on issues relating to public policy on economic security. The organization of COLISE has been modified, with a plenary format bringing together the relevant cabinet directors once every six months, and a restricted format, bringing together more regularly the ministerial advisors whose remit concerns specific cases of economic security. CORIE's actions and decisions are based on the unified economic security reference framework drawn up by SISSE, which includes three classified lists: a list of entities to be protected as a priority; a list of critical technologies; and a list of research units to be protected.

Secondly, at intelligence service level, a Comité d'orientation du renseignement d'intérêt économique (CORIE) has been set up. This committee is co-chaired by the CISSE and the economic and financial affairs advisor to the national intelligence and counter-terrorism coordinator (CNRLT). Meeting on a quarterly basis, this committee aims to facilitate relations between economically competent administrations and the State's intelligence community, since all six specialized intelligence services are represented on it. CORIE's action is thus in line with the national intelligence strategy (SNR) and the national intelligence orientation plan (PNOR), which include a section dedicated to economic intelligence. Economic intelligence was one of the intelligence priorities, as demonstrated by the creation of an economic intelligence directorate within the General Directorate for External Security (DGSE).

In addition, the French Intelligence Act has authorized specialized intelligence services to gather information relating to major economic, industrial and scientific interests. The priority given to economic security and intelligence partly explains the absence of an offensive economic intelligence culture and practices. The State's efforts to structure its economic security and intelligence activities, and to set up new consultation and decision-making structures, are to be commended. This new governance is necessary if we are to overcome a certain naivety about economic intelligence, and enable specialized services, administrations and political leaders to develop their skills in this area. However, it should be remembered that economic security, of which economic intelligence is a component, is not the same as economic intelligence. Indeed, economic security activities exclude, in particular, intelligence and influence activities, which are essential components of economic intelligence activities.

In other words, the implementation of a public economic security policy reflects an essentially defensive vision of economic intelligence, whereas it is felt that advanced economies should adopt a more offensive policy in this area. While some administrative departments do report that they are taking offensive action in the field of economic intelligence, this action remains insufficient and should be extended to more territories and economic operators, and not just to large companies seeking to win major contracts in foreign markets.

It should be noted that the various attempts to structure business intelligence policy have suffered from a lack of political support and stability. Several observations can be made. Firstly, while there is no consensus on the most appropriate administrative organization model, there is a collective recognition that business intelligence issues have been insufficiently taken into account due to the absence of a perennial structure. As a result, several organizational models have been tried and tested, without the public policy of economic intelligence managing to stabilize or find a permanent organization within the State. Since the creation of the CCSE, the many successive changes in the names and administrative forms of the entities responsible for economic intelligence at central level illustrate the difficulty the concept has had in finding an appropriate and lasting position within the State apparatus. The multiplication of structures, the coexistence of entities dedicated to business intelligence - and the resulting lack of coherence and communication - have not helped to stabilize an effective public policy of business intelligence. Secondly, we must also consider that there has not been sufficiently continuous political support to enable business intelligence to become a genuine public policy. Difficulties in communicating with the country's highest political authorities on specific business intelligence issues and cases, as well as the lack of strategic information sharing, have greatly complicated the role of successive business intelligence managers and delegates.

In order to overcome the difficulties outlined during the hearings, and to enable business intelligence to be considered as a genuine public policy, it is essential to create a permanent structure, whose existence would be guaranteed by legislation, and whose organizational procedures would be specified by regulation. The aim is to avoid media hype, and to ensure continuity in the recognition of business intelligence issues, even if the importance attached to them varies from one government to the next. Without wishing to call into question the existing governance of economic security and intelligence, the existence of a permanent, inter-ministerial, multi-disciplinary structure dedicated to economic intelligence is necessary today. We recommend the creation of a General Secretariat for Economic Intelligence (SGIE), whose Secretary General would have both a political and administrative role, on the model of the General Secretariat for European Affairs (SGAE). The Secretary General should also be an advisor to the Head of Government on economic intelligence issues, and have a direct line of communication with the President's office, so as to be able to inform, alert and react rapidly to any cases that may arise.

It is essential that the SGIE has its own multi-disciplinary team to cover all the dimensions of economic intelligence. To facilitate its inter-ministerial coordination work, the SGIE could rely on a network of ministerial economic intelligence correspondents, who should be the same as the ministerial standardization correspondents. Finally, drawing on the lessons of past experience, a direct link should exist between the SGIE and the MEFs. This is why it is also recommended that the head of the SISSE at the DGE should also be a deputy at the SGIE.

Recommendation no. 10: Give the task of steering the national economic intelligence strategy to a General Secretariat for Economic Intelligence (SGIE), whose continuity would be guaranteed by its inclusion in the law. This SGIE should have the following characteristics: be staffed by a dedicated multidisciplinary team; be headed by a Secretary General who would also be an advisor to the Head of Government on economic intelligence issues, on the model of the General Secretariat for European Affairs (SGAE); have a deputy to the SGIE who would be the head of the Strategic Information and Economic Security Department (SISSE) to ensure effective coordination with the economic security policy steered by the Economic and Financial Ministries (MEF); have relays within each ministry with ministerial correspondents for economic intelligence and standardization.

According to the governance established by the decree, the regional prefect, supported by his regional affairs secretariat (SGAR), is responsible for coordinating and implementing the public economic security policy (PPSE) at territorial level. Under his authority, regional delegates for strategic information and economic security (DISSE) belonging to a network led by the SISSE are responsible for coordinating the implementation of the PPSE. In a methodological roadmap, the Ministry of the Interior recommends reinforcing the territorial coordination of the PPSE through simplified, operational governance. It stipulates that the head of the department should appoint a departmental economic security referent, whose mission is to identify local strategic issues, report any threats or vulnerabilities to DISSE or SGAR, and raise awareness of economic security among the general public and economic players. In practice, these referents are usually sub-prefects or the prefect's chief of staff.

With the support of the DISSEs, the departmental economic security referents are also responsible for organizing and leading the departmental economic security committees (CDSEs), which bring together intelligence services and other departments responsible for economic security once or twice a year. These operational meetings enable the department's sensitive entities to be monitored as closely as possible, in order to identify alerts, coordinate the departmental economic security policy, identify new strategic entities, plan awareness-raising actions and initiate any remedial measures required. At regional level, a Regional Economic Security Committee - CRSE) meets once a year under the chairmanship of the regional prefect to bring together the government services responsible for economic security (departmental referents in prefectures, intelligence services, gendarmerie, DISSE, ANSSI) and those involved in its implementation (regional government economic services: DRAAF, DRARI, DREAL, DRFiP, DRDDI, DREETS, ARS) in order to set up an alert detection network for companies and laboratories in the region.

Under the authority of the regional prefect, numerous government departments contribute to the implementation of this PPSE on several sectoral levels. In each department, the DISSEs draw up and update a list of strategic entities, including companies, laboratories and research and innovation ecosystems. This list is broader than the list of companies and research units to be protected as a matter of priority maintained by the SISSE at national level: it includes entities detected as having a significant strategic character by local economic security players due to their mastery of key know-how or technology, their place in the subcontracting chain of a strategic sector, their growth potential or their level of innovation.

Threefold attached to the SGAR, the DREETS and the SISSE, the DISSEs perform valuable work in identifying and transmitting information. However, it is regrettable that the DISSEs are few in number, which means that they are unable to cover all the diversity and complexity of our territories. In addition, other government departments not specifically responsible for economic security contribute to the implementation of this PPSE. The General Directorate for Internal Security (DGSI) monitors, raises awareness of and advises companies and training and research institutes on the risks of foreign interference, often via one or two regional offices at departmental level. Another intelligence service, the Defense Security Intelligence Division – DRSD -, is responsible for counter-intelligence in the defense sector, and mobilizes regional teams to raise alerts about companies in the defense industrial and technological base (BITD). The SCRT (Central Service for Territorial Intelligence - Central Territorial Intelligence Service), attached to the national police force, also carries out economic security missions, meeting with company directors, union leaders and employees, and reporting information and social alerts on possible destabilization of an employment area.

The French national agency for information systems security (ANSSI) also has regional delegates. They help to prevent incidents and raise awareness of good IT security practices among local public and private players. Within the French National Gendarmerie's General Directorate (DGGN), the SECOPE (Economic Security and Company Protection) sections play an important role at regional level in raising awareness among local businesses, and particularly among small and medium-sized enterprises (SMEs), for whom a SECOPE visit is often their first encounter with the notion of economic security. In 2022: visits to companies to raise awareness of threats to economic and industrial interests were carried out;

local company awareness conferences and 6 national conferences were organized.

The vast majority of these awareness-raising and exchange visits are very well received by managers, who have very little information on the subject and relay many concerns that they generally feel powerless to address. SECOPE's work extends right down to the smallest company - one that may be involved because it is strategic to an employment area, another because it supplies a major group with a product that is essential to the value chain. SECOPE's action is therefore essential, both in terms of reporting alerts, identifying new potentially sensitive companies, instituting defensive reflexes and, more broadly, contributing to the dissemination of a culture of economic security. Last but not least, the establishment in certain regions of economic security referents within regional directorates, such as the regional directorates for customs and indirect rights (DRDDI), public finance (DRFiP) or the SCRT, shows that they make information exchange even more fluid, by acting as privileged contacts within their administration for DISSE and other administrations in charge of PPSE. In this respect, the appointment of economic security referents should be systematized in all decentralized administrations in charge of economic and financial missions.

In all cases, the successful implementation of a national business intelligence strategy at local level requires sufficient human and financial resources to enable government officials to carry out their duties properly, especially when business intelligence is added to the missions normally entrusted to these administrations. The prefectures have not been sufficiently mobilized in the field of business intelligence, although this varies from region to region and from department to department. That's why they want to reassert the prefectural level as a strategic lever for implementing the national economic intelligence strategy (SNIE). Finally, while the region remains the leader in terms of economic development, the departmental level is essential in terms of economic intelligence to ensure close monitoring of the local economic fabric. The implementation of a national economic intelligence strategy (SNIE) at territorial level is based on the effective dissemination of an economic intelligence culture through cooperation between government departments and local authorities, and in particular the regions, which have the lead in economic matters. Involving local authorities more closely in economic intelligence policy would make it possible to reconcile the economic security policy currently implemented under the authority of the regional prefect with economic development, which falls within the remit of the regional council, to develop a genuine economic intelligence approach with both defensive and offensive aspects.

The need to involve local authorities has already been expressed: a circular reminded regional prefects of the need to involve regional councils in work aimed at reinforcing economic security in the regions. In practice, this involvement took the form of the State-Region partnership charter on territorial economic intelligence and economic security, which called for a regional strategic committee to be set up at least once a year, bringing together representatives of government departments, local authorities, economic operators, research and business. In some regions, this committee has taken the form of a strategic territorial economic intelligence committee (CRIET) co-chaired by the regional prefect and the president of the regional council, bringing together all regional economic intelligence players: intelligence services, DISSE, regional ANSSI delegates, regional council, chambers of commerce and industry, competitive clusters, universities, etc.

However, not all local authorities have set up such committees, nor do they meet annually. Nor do annual CRIETs replace day-to-day cooperation: today, local authorities do not take part in the departmental economic security committees run by DISSE and the departmental economic security referent. They are therefore limited in their operational monitoring of sensitive entities in their area. To remedy this situation, some territories have set up ad hoc bodies where the region and government departments cooperate. Other advances testify to the growing awareness of the need for cooperation between the State and the regions in the field of economic security. The partnership charter provides for the circulation of information between the State and the regions through the joint development of an active alert and monitoring system, enabling the circulation of information between regional prefects and local authorities; training and the development of a shared culture through joint awareness-raising and training initiatives aimed at the territorial agents concerned, the joint organization of meetings for economic players, and the conduct of any reflection leading to the emergence and consolidation of a shared culture of territorial economic intelligence and, in particular, economic security, and the development of shared tools - for example, secure information exchange systems, analysis grids or a common confidentiality reference framework; analysis and forecasting through the dissemination of notes, summaries, analyses and diagnoses; organization and implementation of ongoing dialogue.

At central level, an annual meeting will be held between representatives of the ministries concerned and the regions. At regional level, regional prefects and presidents of regional councils will co-chair a regional strategy committee at least once a year, bringing together representatives of government departments, local authorities, economic operators, research and business. To strengthen State-region cooperation in the service of the SNIE, systematize the creation in each region of a regional economic intelligence committee (CRIE), which could have two formations: a plenary formation, co-chaired by the regional prefects and the presidents of the regional councils. It would meet at least once a year, and would be attended by all economic intelligence players; a restricted formation, dedicated to economic security, which would involve the regional council and meet more frequently on operational subjects, in particular threats to local businesses. This CRIE would oversee the regional implementation of the PPIE (public policy on economic intelligence), and would bring together representatives from government departments, local authorities, economic operators, research and business.

While the regions are increasingly taking on board the challenges of economic intelligence, in line with the law's recognition of the region's role as leader in the field of economic development, the extent to which they are doing so varies from one region to another. Some regions, given their economic fabric and geography, have historically been very active in the field of economic intelligence. A number of best practices have been implemented in these regions, and would benefit from being shared with other local authorities. Some regions have a well-established industry. In addition to their regional and departmental economic security committees, they hold annual CRIET meetings with the regional council, and have set up a network of intelligence experts: some twenty players (competitiveness clusters, industry and business representatives, etc.) exchange best practices in the area of intelligence, and share tools where appropriate. The Regional Economic Development Agency also has an Economic and Territorial Intelligence department which regularly produces surveys and can carry out studies on behalf of its shareholders, i.e. the Region and its intercommunal bodies.

Other regions stand out for their high concentration of industrial sites belonging to major groups. The industrial sector accounts for 20% of regional added value, while 36% of regional GDP is devoted to exports. These regions have been selected as pilot regions for Territorial Economic Intelligence. This has led to the creation of an Economic Intelligence Strategy and Forecasting mission (SPIE), reporting to the Deputy General Manager for the Economy, with the aim of integrating economic intelligence in an operational and cross-functional way into all the subjects it deals with. This mission produces alert notes on emerging topics, analysis notes and a weekly intelligence bulletin. The region's economic intelligence system is also based on a more proactive economic development dimension, supported by the Development Agency, which helps new companies to set up in the region by assisting with investment programs and job creation. An export team has also been set up under a partnership agreement.

As business intelligence is a network issue, government departments and local authorities must work hand in hand with local economic players - consular bodies and competitiveness clusters in particular - to promote a shared business intelligence culture. At present, the network of Chambers of Commerce and Industry (CCI) does not have a business intelligence strategy. However, the involvement of the consular networks had enabled the appropriation of business intelligence practices and principles within the territory. The contract of objectives and performance signed between the network of chambers of commerce and industry (CCI) and the French government provides for a number of actions to promote economic security in the regions, but does not include either economic intelligence or economic security as a specific component. These actions concern the appointment of referents in the regions, the participation of CCIs in meetings organized by ANSSI in the regions, and participation in the cybersecurity alert system.

In addition to Chambers of Commerce and Industry, other local economic players are involved in the implementation of a business intelligence strategy, such as competitive clusters and technology acceleration and transfer companies (SATTs), which play an important role in the valorization of research. SATTs are set up by a number of public institutions, notably universities and research laboratories, to transform inventions from public research into innovations for companies. They act as a one-stop shop for technology transfer and competitiveness in a given region. The French Minister for Higher Education and Research had announced the appointment of an economic security advisor, empowered to protect national defense secrets, by the President of each SATT (Technology Transfer Acceleration Company). This network of referents is coordinated by the DISSEs and DRARIs at regional level. Competitiveness clusters, which bring together companies, research laboratories and educational establishments in a given region, represent another category of key players in the field of research, particularly applied research. They support collaborative research and innovation projects. They therefore play an important role in promoting and advising young innovative companies on economic intelligence, although the heterogeneity of their practices has been highlighted. Although the specifications for the labeling of competitiveness clusters mention the need to take into account the challenges of protecting scientific and technical potential, particularly in terms of economic security and the protection of the most sensitive information, the State could be encouraged to strengthen the economic intelligence activities of these clusters - by appointing an economic intelligence referent, developing personalized strategic intelligence monitoring for the companies supported, etc.

As a reminder, as early as 1994, low awareness of business intelligence was identified as an obstacle to its dissemination and to the construction of a high-performance business intelligence system. Indeed, business intelligence is rarely detached from a business skill, and struggles to spread within companies and administrations as a common culture. Today, continuous training in business intelligence is still not a reflex for managers in both the public and private sectors. However, the range of courses on offer has grown considerably since the early days of business intelligence, with the The Graduate Institute of National Defense (IHEDN) organizing specific training courses, the School of Economic Warfare (EGE) and the Graduate Institute of the Ministry of the Interior (IHEMI). IHEDN's training courses include annual cycles, three times a year, covering everything from intelligence and compliance to cybersecurity and economic security. At the same time, shorter, thematic courses are organized, as well as regional sessions. The single national session includes a major in defense and economic security, particularly targeted at high-level managers in the public and private sectors.

EGE offers continuing education courses in strategic management and business intelligence, cybersecurity and risk management, as well as certification programs open to all. The IHEMI offers business intelligence training tailored to different audiences: some courses are aimed at government executives, elected representatives, security force representatives, freelance professionals, trade unions or private-sector executives, such as the "Business Protection and Business Intelligence" course, while others are more general, such as the five-day "From Intelligence to Analysis" module. There is also a module entitled "Economic security referent", designed for economic security referents in competitive clusters and other research and innovation support structures, such as technology transfer accelerator companies (SATT). Today, the General Business Department lists some twenty specialized business intelligence training courses at Masters 1 and 2 level. While underlining the dynamism and growth of the business intelligence training on offer, it is vital that such training be offered on a mass scale, both in universities and prestigious schools, and in both initial and continuing training courses.

Finally, training in standardization, a component of business intelligence, has been in decline for some years. The few general standardization training courses that do exist are little known. There is also a great need for specialized training in the field of standardization. For example, toxicology regulations and standards have a major impact on the activities of companies in the pharmaceutical, cosmetics, agrochemical and chemical sectors. However, in a study carried out for the French Ministry of the Economy, experts highlighted the lack of structured training courses in toxicology, hampering the development of skills and the recognition of the associated professions. The study underlines the concern of manufacturers about the risk of losing competence in this field as expertise is reduced.

Within the State, if the administrations concerned by the implementation of the PPSE are sensitized to economic security - and not to a more global economic intelligence approach - this sensitization is linked to the job, whereas it should be inter-ministerial and irrigate all the State's fields of action. In particular, within the Treasury's international network of economic departments in many countries around the world, reporting on strategic economic information should be part of public servants' duties. However, there is no training specifically dedicated to economic intelligence for those working in the economic services.

Within companies, economic intelligence is far from being systematically taken into account: beyond strategic companies and Operators of Vital Interest (OIV), economic intelligence is rarely a factor in the company's thinking, particularly for SMEs, which can nevertheless be the target of foreign influences. Alerts from the DGGN's local teams regularly bring to light cases of SMEs with little or no awareness, despite the fact that they play a structuring role for a region, an employment area or a strategic value chain. More broadly, business intelligence awareness should be integrated into all general training modules, in civil service schools, engineering schools and business schools, as well as in all university courses in research, social sciences, international relations and law. The introduction of a two-week training module in economic intelligence at the National School of Administration was a step forward, but was made compulsory only in international courses, i.e. those intended for future foreign civil servants.

It's worth pointing out the low level of cooperation between the State and companies on business intelligence issues, with some companies indicating that they have no connection whatsoever with the public administrations responsible for this area. Similarly, all the expert reports on business intelligence deplore the low level of cooperation between the State and companies on business intelligence issues. This lack of contact can be explained not only by the historical and cultural defiance of the business world and consulting firms, but also by the lack of a clear strategy and long-term governance of business intelligence at government level. Changes in interlocutors and political alternations lead to shifts in the administration's stance towards players and changes in the public authority's prioritization of subjects, which penalize the continuity and quality of exchanges.

And yet, the French State could benefit from the expertise of certain firms specializing in business intelligence. It is surprising to note the ease with which government departments have been able to call on strategic consultancy services for several years without, for example, the Government shareholding agency ever having called on a business intelligence firm to support it in the management of the State shareholder's portfolio, which includes a number of strategic activities. Another way of strengthening cooperation between the State and companies in the field of business intelligence is to include a business intelligence component in the contracts of the Strategic Sector Committees (CSF). These CSFs bring together representatives of the State and local authorities, trade federations representing the entire value chain (upstream and downstream for an industry), employee unions, competitive clusters and business financing organizations, where appropriate specialized. They are ideal forums for the cross-disciplinary dissemination of business intelligence. The CSFs also cover strategic sectors such as digital infrastructure, agrifood, rail, healthcare, nuclear, automotive, mining and metallurgy, etc., most of which are supported by the French government. Including a business intelligence component in the CSFs would therefore enable companies' business intelligence efforts to be anchored in a medium-term strategic vision that coincides with the course set by a public policy that is structuring the economy due to the considerable amount of investment involved.

To promote the dissemination of a business intelligence culture and the sharing of information between the public and private sectors, dedicated meeting places need to be created. A biannual conference bringing together, on a national scale, all the players involved in economic intelligence - local authorities, chambers of commerce and industry, companies, trade unions, government departments and universities - would provide an opportunity to present the progress of the SNIE as well as to highlight the initiatives and best practices of the players involved.

In addition to the development of training, which is essential to the dissemination of a business intelligence culture in both the administrative and entrepreneurial environments, it is important for companies and public authorities alike to be able to rely on a business intelligence industry. In order to strengthen the French business intelligence industry, support for research in this field must be resolute. The number of academic publications on business intelligence is relatively low, despite the fact that business intelligence concerns at least six major disciplines: law (in particular patents, asset and capital protection), political science, economics, computer science, information and communication science, and management science. This relative weakness can be explained by several factors: few scientifically recognized debates empower the corpus of business intelligence, which therefore suffers from the coexistence of several definitions and a lack of recognition; many works may deal with subjects related to business intelligence without expressly naming it - economic intelligence, economic security, or more specific subjects such as intercultural management, normative influence or foreign investment control.

To recognize business intelligence as a subject of study in its own right, a national business intelligence research program should be set up, with dedicated doctoral research grants that can be applied to the many disciplines to which business intelligence refers - law, management, political science, IT, etc. Encouraging research into business intelligence should also involve the economic fabric itself, which will benefit from it: local authorities and companies, particularly SMEs and ETIs, can use industrial research training agreements (CIFRE) to entrust a PhD student with a business intelligence research topic. However, few local authorities, which are eligible for the scheme, currently make use of CIFREs, most of which are still signed by private companies. In order not to miss the technological turning point in business intelligence, this support for research must not overlook artificial intelligence (AI) systems, which can be used to collect, process and disseminate business information.

The business intelligence industry is structured around a number of emerging players, but is still lagging behind the much more developed Anglo-Saxon compliance ecosystem, which is worrying in two respects. On the one hand, the number of standards with extraterritorial scope is increasing, making compliance a growing concern for companies. Against this backdrop, internal audits are on the increase within companies, to guard against breaches or as part of post-sanction monitoring of compliance with extraterritorial standards. During these operations, companies need the support of expert firms. On the other hand, compliance professionals are also key players in the dissemination of a culture of business intelligence - through the provision of targeted services for SMEs and large corporations alike: many consulting and auditing firms now offer, in addition to their compliance activities, forensics or business intelligence services that combine prevention, risk management and remediation, all with a view to complying with the various legislative and regulatory requirements to which companies are subject in financial or extra-financial matters; law firms also support the same companies in these same areas. While Anglo-Saxon law firms are the main contacts for multinationals, given their size and network, the legal departments of local companies also have an interest in using independent firms, not least to avoid any conflicts of interest. These medium-sized firms could also be attractive to ETIs and SMEs, for whom they can develop tailored offerings.

Financial and non-financial rating agencies assess the performance of companies and local authorities in order to provide information to investors. In the financial sector, three companies, now all controlled by American entities, dominate the market with 91% market share: S&P Global Ratings, Moody's and Fitch. Their ratings, which are closely followed by international investors, can tarnish the reputation of a country or worsen the situation of a company. The European agencies, of which there are almost thirty, are struggling to establish themselves: a regulation encourages issuers who use at least two agencies to use one with a market share of less than 10%. Since the regulation is not binding - it simply stipulates that if the issuer does not use a CRA with a total market share of less than 10%, this must be documented - this provision has not undermined the dominance of American agencies. Yet, according to the European Securities and Markets Authority (ESMA), the application of this regulation would reduce market concentration by 40% and support European players who are not currently referenced by the European Central Bank, which only recognizes the ratings issued by the Big Three to assess the counterparties provided by Eurobanks.

-Local certification bodies are fairly well established. These players need to be supported in the face of the hegemony of Anglo-Saxon players. Today, the normative threat is particularly strong, as our partner- competitors have the means to impose coercive standards on our companies. In this respect, an in-depth national compliance ecosystem (including specialized law firms) will enable companies to better adapt and prevent risks. To encourage the use of these players, public authorities have a role to play in communicating with companies. To make business intelligence a shared culture, we need to involve companies, national and local public authorities, as well as the general public. To achieve this, it is essential to reiterate the concrete, patriotic dimension of economic intelligence: in a globalized context where states are waging a veritable economic war against each other, promoting local companies and their know-how, and preserving their jobs, is a patriotic commitment. It's a message that needs to be built up and relayed by the public authorities, so that economic intelligence becomes part of everyone's practices, and becomes a reflex.

It is therefore important to mobilize citizens in a very concrete way around the challenges of economic intelligence. Young people could be mobilized and made aware of business intelligence during the Universal National Service, which is open to all volunteers between the ages of 15 and 17: during the first phase, which includes a collective stay with various activity modules, the defense, security and national resilience module could address business intelligence issues. In addition, the IHEDN organizes an annual national training session for members of parliament and public and private decision-makers, whose list is made public and who benefit from comprehensive training in business intelligence issues. Smaller but more numerous regional sessions are also organized. Specialized training courses in economic and strategic intelligence (IES) are available for operational managers and executives of companies and institutions. These training sessions therefore build up a particularly interesting pool of people voluntarily trained in business intelligence, whose skills it would be a pity to deprive ourselves of.

It would therefore be advisable to continue to mobilize these people once they have completed their training, on a voluntary basis, by involving them in a national economic intelligence reserve: its mission would be to disseminate the culture and practices of economic intelligence (to the media, administrations, businesses), to act as a receptacle for alerts and, if necessary, to be mobilized to support other organizations on more operational missions, for example in cybersecurity. The reserve would also be open to any other volunteers trained in business intelligence.

Printed in Poland
by Amazon Fulfillment
Poland Sp. z o.o., Wrocław